1-13-10

MW00441303

RIDING THE HOLLYWOOD TRAIL II:

BLAZING THE EARLY TELEVISION TRAIL

I hope you
enjoy these trails too!

Your
Pal,

Charlie
Le Sueur

RIDING THE HOLLYWOOD TRAIL II:

BLAZING THE EARLY TELEVISION TRAIL

BY

CHARLIE LeSUEUR

THE AUTHOR

 Charlie and his wife, Dawn, reside in his hometown of Mesa, Arizona where he divides his time between being the performing arts director for Sequoia Star Academy, teaching a class on the history of western film at Central Arizona College and film acting.

When not teaching and acting, Charlie is either on the road traveling throughout the United States as a guest at Western Film Festivals or writing on different aspects on western film and television.

In January, 2014, Charlie was honored to have his 'bootprints' added alongside those of Peter Brown, Clint Walker, Michael Dante, Jock Mahoney, Robert Fuller and many others that he grew up watching on film and television. In February of the same year he officially became Arizona's Official Western Film Historian.

This book, or parts thereof, may not be reproduced in any form with out prior written permission from the author or publisher.

ISBN-13: - 978-0-9962483-4-1   Paper
ISBN-10: - 099624834X
ISBN-13: - 978-0-9962483-5-8   E
ISBN-10: - 0996248358

© Copyright 2015 by Charles LeSueur, All Rights Reserved

Timber Creek Press
Imprint of Timber Creek Productions, LLC
312 N. Commerce St.
Gainesville, Texas

Contact Us:
Published by: Timber Creek Press
timbercreekpresss@yahoo.com
www.timbercreekpress.net
www.facebook.com/TimberCreekPress

DEDICATION and ACKNOWLEDGMENTS

This book is once again Dedicated to my Dad who always had the TV Westerns on even during dinnertime and to my Mother who always let him.

Other acknowledgments go to:

Johnny Western for putting the thought in my head to start writing, and to Buck Taylor giving me the title for my first book.

To Marshall Terrill whose advice and encouragement helped me continue.

To Larry John, and Mary and Jim Brown who aligned all the stars back in 1991 to make it happen in the first place.

To Donna Wilmeth and Cindy Mitchum who have given me new homes for my talents.

To great friends, Alex Cord, Michael and Mary Jane Dante, Cheryl Rogers-Barnett, Larry Barnett, Don Kay Reynolds, and Tony Gill for their help and vital information.

To Ken Farmer, who was just what I needed to help me get this done.

To Dawn for years of patience.

To the one and only, Robert Fuller who, for whatever reason, has given me his friendship and a constant amount of fun.

A special thanks to Buck Montgomery for the front cover.

There are literally hundreds I have forgotten, but there will be other books.

ENDORSEMENTS

When it comes to western movies and the guys who starred in them, Charlie LeSueur is the ultimate authority, a walking encyclopedia. For guys like me who grew up on the Saturday matinees his knowledge and information enriches the priceless memories of my fantasies in the saddle going ninety miles an hour on a sure-footed steed. One of my favorites was "Wild Bill Elliot." He always seemed like the real deal. Good wardrobe, great looking horses, either a dappled gray or a buckskin, is what I remember. He rode well and wore a good hat. If you're a fan on the level that I am, his book is a treasure, you will learn so much.
Alex Cord

Charlie and I go way back. He's been the host of many Q&A panels I've been on. Bobby Hoy and I have enjoyed working with him at many different festivals because he brings great stories out of the actors. I thought the fans at The High Chaparral Reunion couldn't be beat for what they know about my career, but Charlie never fails to bring up something no one has ever asked about. He wouldn't just ask about the movies I made with John Wayne—he'd ask about guest stars that I worked with on "Outlaws" back in the early 60's that I'd almost forgotten about! Charlie really knows his stuff."
Don Collier

Take a deep seat and a tight rein. If you thought Riding the Hollywood Trail 1 was riveting and informative, wait until you read Riding the Hollywood Trail ll: Blazing the Early Television Trail. Charlie takes you on a ride through the early days of Western movies to the early days of Western television, with the cowboy stars and sidekicks you know so well, as well

as the trials and tribulations the stars had with their studio bosses who made some of them miserable and some of them millions. Charlie describes the move from the big screen to the small screen with his expert research and knowledge that he has shown so many times before. Just when you thought you knew the true story, Charlie says "Whoa!" and tells you what really happened. That's what makes Charlie's books so interesting. It's a can't put down book! Enjoy.
Robert Fuller

Having been on many Question & Answer panels and even hosting a few of them myself at the Western Legends Roundup in Kanab, Utah I can honestly say that Charlie makes being on one a real pleasure. His knowledge and quick wit is enjoyed by us celebrities and the audience alike and it is always great fun for me and something to look forward to. So I know you will enjoy this book for sure!!
Peter Brown

In Riding the Hollywood Trail: Tales of the Silver Screen Cowboys, Charlie LeSueur brought you the stories of the "B" Western cowboy film pioneers from the silent era to the end of the trail with the coming of television. In Blazing the Television Trail, Charlie continues the story as a select few cowpokes successfully made the switch to early television while others had a tough go of it. Gene, Hoppy, Roy, The Lone Ranger, The Cisco Kid, Gabby Hayes, Lash LaRue, and Red Ryder are just a few whose stories are brought to life, with plenty of behind the scenes intrigue. Enjoy the Trail!
"Charlie LeSueur hosts a Q &A panel for actors and actresses better than anyone I know. His knowledge of the western genre is as good as it gets. This book is a must read".
Michael Dante

OTHER NOVELS FROM
TIMBER CREEK PRESS

MILITARY ACTION/TECHNO
BLACK EAGLE FORCE: Eye of the Storm (Book #1)
by Buck Stienke and Ken Farmer
www.tinyurl.com/storm4un
BLACK EAGLE FORCE: Sacred Mountain (Book #2)
by Buck Stienke and Ken Farmer
www.tinyurl.com/SacMtn2
RETURN of the STARFIGHTER (Book #3)
by Buck Stienke and Ken Farmer
www.tinyurl.com/StarF01
BLACK EAGLE FORCE: BLOOD IVORY (Book #4)
by Buck Stienke and Ken Farmer with Doran Ingrham
www.tinyurl.com/befivory
BLACK EAGLE FORCE: FOURTH REICH (Book #5)
By Buck Stienke and Ken Farmer
www.tinyurl.com/befreich
BLOOD BROTHERS - Doran Ingrham, Buck Stienke
and Ken Farmer
www.tinyurl.com/bloodbrothers1
DARK SECRET - Doran Ingrham
http://tinyurl.com/darksecret-2
BLACK STAR BAY by T.C. Miller
Http://amzn.to/1oYSFO6

HISTORICAL FICTION WESTERN
THE NATIONS by Ken Farmer and Buck Stienke
www.tinyurl.com/the-nations-Bass
HAUNTED FALLS by Ken Farmer and Buck Stienke
Www.tinyurl.com/haunted-falls-Bass
HELL HOLE by Ken Farmer
Www.tinyurl.com/hell-hole-Bass3
ACROSS the RED by Ken Farmer and Buck Stienke
Www.tinyurl.com/AcrossRed
DEVIL'S CANYON by Buck Stienke
http://tinyurl.com/devils-canyon-B

Coming Soon

MILITARY ACTION/TECHNO
BLACK EAGLE FORCE: ISIS by Buck Stienke and Ken Farmer
BLACK STAR MOUNTAIN by T.C. Miller

HISTORICAL FICTION WESTERN
BASS and the LADY by Ken Farmer & Buck Stienke
Book five of the Bass Reeves Saga

TIMBER CREEK PRESS

Musings from the Author

When I wrote *Riding the Hollywood Trail: Tales of the Silver Screen Cowboys* I did so with the thought of writing a book on the history of the "B" western stars that I would like to read. I believe I did just that and—hopefully—those of you who read it feel the same way.

With this volume it seemed like the next step would be to talk about the early days of television westerns, primarily the ones starring our silver screen heroes. For some film cowpokes it was a smooth transition, for others it was a bumpy ride, and for others it never really panned out.

Gene Autry, being the businessman he was, plotted his move to television while still maintaining a high profile in movie theaters. Roy Rogers, on the other hand, had a long court battle with Republic Pictures for his right to make the move to the small screen. He finally succeeded but it would be a bittersweet victory.

William Boyd was in a class all by himself. He took a fictional character and made it his for all time. Gene would always be Gene, Roy was always Roy, and Bill Boyd forever more would be Hopalong Cassidy. With television they were easily accessible to fans to enjoy in the privacy of their home. Some like Lash LaRue and Monte Hale suffered from not having such an intimate association with their fans, while others like Russell Hayden moved into early television production with syndicated westerns.

This volume covers the pioneers of television oaters from 1949 to 1955, the year when televised westerns grew up with *The Life and Legend of Wyatt Earp*, *Cheyenne* and *Gunsmoke*.

By 1958, Gene, Roy, Hoppy, Cisco, and The Lone Ranger reruns had been, for the most part, relegated to Saturday mornings—a slot they would fill much to the delight of kids for the next decade.

For some of us television would be our introduction to these transitional heroes. It was a magical time when we would sit in front of the black and white TV set and believe that Roy and Dale where platonic friends who lived in Mineral City, that a jaded cowpoke would actually believe a man who wears a mask and travels with an Indian companion was actually a hero without much convincing, or that a flamboyantly costumed Latin hero could fend for himself alongside his grammar fracturing sidekick.

In other words it was an innocent time when we were told that in case of an atom bomb blast we would be saved if we ducked under our school desk or in a door way. We believed in magic and heroes. Ever since that was taken away from us the world has been worse for it.

So let's return to those years for just a while. Some of us will be reliving these wonderful frontier memories while others will be exposed to them for the first time.

No matter which group you fall into I hope you enjoy *Riding the Old Hollywood Trail, Volume II* as much as I did writing it. It's been a real labor of love.

***

CHAPTER ONE

In the Beginning

The genesis of television has its roots going all the way back to 1873, but for our purposes we're going to jump ahead just a few years to 1928 when Philo T. Farnsworth was able to transmit one single visible line at his laboratory in San Francisco. That same year the Federal Radio Commissioner C.F. Jenkins broadcast from an experimental station just outside of Washington D.C., while a station in New York City began limited live broadcasts.

The prediction was that by 1929 there would be television available to the public. It seemed it would come true when General Electric and RCA began limited television broadcasts in 1928 and '29. The big push for 7 day per week television broadcasting came in 1931 when the General Broadcasting System and the Columbia Broadcasting System started general programming from New York City. That same year a station was opened in Los Angeles. The programming was limited to be sure but it seemed that TV was on its way. So what happened?

It gets a bit complicated at this point. Needless to say, many stations would start and stop during the decade. One problem was that there wasn't any real sponsorship to keep these experimental television stations up and running and viewer ship would obviously be extremely limited.

Advertising on the tube began in 1941 when NBC affiliate WNBT simply broadcast a test pattern modified to look like a clock with the words "Bulova Watch Time." Throughout the next two decades Bulovia watch time would be a popular catch phrase at NBC. This event was followed by a live broadcast of a Brooklyn Dodgers game from Ebbets Field.

World War II curtailed the advancement of television when the Federal Communications Commission limited commercial air time to 4 hours per week. As the war geared down in 1944 NBC began linking networks in New York, Washington D.C. and Philadelphia.

The Dumont Television Network started in 1946, while CBS and NBC stepped up programming in 1948. Because television licensing was starting to boom in the first years after the war, in 1948 the FCC put a freeze on anymore networks starting up which would be upheld until 1952. At the time there were fewer than 50,000 households with a TV set.

This is a very simplistic history of television. To cover all the intricacies would take the entire book. It's an interesting history but we're here to talk about westerns and their place in television history. You'll find – as if you didn't know – that they were definitely the pioneers of the television plains in inventiveness.

Just like the part they played at our local theaters they were up against villains in real life that would have them fail at further television success. But just like they did on the silver screen they would dominate the small screen in the family living room for almost another 20 years.

It couldn't have come at a more perfect time. The major film studios were being forced to divest themselves of movie theater ownership. The eventual downfall of the contract system led to more producers, studios and actors looking to television.

Each of the "Big Three" western stars Gene, Roy, and William Boyd had their own reasons for going into television. Boyd had already seen how his older Hopalong Cassidy films could bring even more revenue and untold wealth through editing them for TV. Being a shrewd businessman he could see the only way to head was into a new set of adventures for Hoppy on TV.

Gene would be the only one of the three to release theatrical features while doing his TV show. He was probably the most theater friendly. He convinced studios and theater owners that his TV series were really "Mini-Movies," slick advertisements, for his films being shown in their theaters.

Roy Rogers desperately wanted out of his contract with Herbert J. Yates at Republic Pictures. Yates let him appear on **The Gabby Hayes Show** in 1950 as a nod to Roy's old sidekick, and hoping it would convince Roy to sign a new contract with the studio in 1951.

Roy even thanked his boss on the show for letting him appear. But it would prove to be a onetime peace offering. *"I can't imagine Dad thanking Yates unless he was told to."* Roy's daughter Cheryl Rogers-Barnett would tell me when I emailed her on the appearance. Yates hoped the cowboy star would have been more agreeable to renew his contract, never the less Roy refused to sign unless he could do his own TV show independently of Republic Pictures. The dispute would cause Roy no end of problems before it was eventually settled.

The other cowboy pioneers were characters with no specific identity before coming to TV. The Cisco Kid had been popular in films for different studios and 4 different actors.

The welcome mat was obviously wearing thin for the character on screen by the time it hit television. The last theatrical release would set the template for Duncan Renaldo and Leo Carrillo to find sudden late career fame beyond their belief.

The Lone Ranger had only sporadic popularity on the big screen through two mediocre serials not representative of the character. The Ranger's popularity had been a lengthy one on radio, and would pick up millions of new fans with Clayton Moore's TV and film interpretation—one that would never be equaled on screen to date.

Cowboys would rule the airwaves until more powerful villains in charge of programming decided they were no longer a viable product for rating demographics. According to them the very kids who had grown up watching westerns now wanted something different, something hip.

Fortunately, we now have several venues to watch our heroes ride across the plains and introduce them to the generations to come. Who knows, someday they may be watching Roy, Gene, Hoppy, Cisco, and The Lone Ranger via a hologram in sen-surround—reference to the '70s.

Until then enjoy the history of our cowboy stars as they made the jump from the big to small screen.

***

CHAPTER TWO

History Repeating Itself

By 1927 the Hollywood film industry was all abuzz wondering how to handle this new thing called "Talkies." Many studios couldn't decide whether to switch to sound right away, do it gradually, or just ignore it all together hoping it was just a fad.

Ironically, the larger studios felt the heat just as much if not more than the smaller independent releasing companies. They had reason to worry, for while the independent studios didn't have money invested in larger than life stars, the majors had big name actors under contract.

Within 5 years of the switch to sound big stars like John Gilbert, Buster Keaton, Theda Bara and Clara Bow had lost their shine. It could be due to unacceptable voices, unable to adapt to dialogue, accents that didn't qualify them for the all-American parts they'd been playing, difficulty in changing their acting style, or simply retiring from the screen. The studios rushed to get stars from the stage, but even that brought problems with too theatrical a style.

Some stars easily made the change and became even bigger stars. Actors like Gary Cooper, Laurel and Hardy, Greta Garbo, and William Boyd continued to thrive because they had the style and voices that would accentuate their status.

Western stars like Ken Maynard, Tom Mix, Tim McCoy, Buck Jones and Hoot Gibson would successfully continue into the sound era, though they were for the most part extremely limited in the acting department. Maynard would even introduce music to the western genre.

Despite the fact that it seemed at first that westerns might have a problem with the coming of sound, it was soon found that it could be done in an easy and satisfactory, for the most part, way for the time.

The major producers and directors soon created classics such as *In Old Arizona* (1928) with Warner Baxter as the first 'talking' Cisco Kid, *The Virginian* (1929) with an up and coming actor by the name of Gary Cooper, and *The Big Trail* (1930) with a hopeful John Wayne. Baxter, Cooper, and Wayne had all been active on screen since 1914, 1923, and 1926 respectively with Baxter and Cooper already known commodities by the coming of sound. Wayne, on the other hand, was handed his first starring role in talkies by none other than well-known director Raoul Walsh. Ironically, Walsh was to star as the Cisco Kid in *In Old Arizona,* but an unfortunate accident caused him to lose an eye during shooting.

The part then went to "B" cowboy Buddy Roosevelt who broke his leg shortly before filming began. The unlikely casting of Baxter as the Mexican bandit would garner him an Oscar for Best Actor.

Both Baxter and Cooper scored in their roles, both of which would later become successful television shows. *The Big Trail* was a flop primarily because of the extensive equipment that the theaters would need to install to show the film in the new wide screen 70mm process known as Fox Grandeur. Ironically Walsh had offered the role to Gary Cooper who turned it down. After this film John Wayne would appear in a handful of "A" productions before becoming a very successful "B" western actor. That would all change in 1939 with the release of *Stagecoach.*

By then Cooper was a huge star and Baxter had appeared as Cisco in three films for major studio 20th Century Fox, ending that same year with *The Return of the Cisco Kid.* As a side-note, Wayne would become a successful star while still having to appear in "B" films for Republic Pictures due to his binding contract with studio head, Herbert J. Yates.

Slowly the major film industry realized that sound was here to stay. Low, low budget companies that specialized in "oaters" where shown it could be done when independent western film maker Leo D. Maloney made the first independent western in 1929, **Overland Bound**. The film was very crude—even by the standards of 1929. By using discarded film stock ends, borrowing equipment, in some cases without anyone's knowledge or approval, Maloney was able to make the film. Maloney had made over 180 films—acting, producing, and directing—before making his sound film. Its successful opening should have opened more doors for Maloney, making him a noted historical film maker. Unfortunately, after its premiere in New York City, Maloney partied a little too hard and died of a heart attack that night. The film is considered to be lost.

However, Maloney set the stage for independent sound westerns and the rest—as they say—is history. Raoul Walsh and Leo Maloney were pioneers of sound film boosting the enjoyment of going to the neighborhood movie theater.

Just 20 years later film would once again be at major crossroads. The difference was that the advent of sound enhanced the theater going experience and brought a larger audience to the movies. However, the new change could quite possibly damage the film industry. This of course would be television. The major studios now had to become inventive to stop people from staying at home. Ironically—just like they did with the beginning of sound—it would be westerns and cowboy stars that successfully showed the way into this new era, proving that both movies and television could thrive together.

But in the beginning the mandate went out from all film studios. None of their actors were to appear on the fledgling medium called television. The threat wasn't without warrant. Having your favorite actors appear for free in your living room would be an appealing change over paying 46 cents to visit the neighborhood movie theater.

Radio had never been a threat to the film industry—far from it. The studios found they could use the audio medium to showcase their stars and publicize their films. Radio and film worked hand in hand and made bigger stars of personalities like Bob Hope, Red Skelton, and Jack Benny.

The Lone Ranger thrived on radio, as well as Tom Mix whose adventures lived on long after the death of the cowboy star, who had never appeared as himself on the radio show anyway. Gene Autry had been broadcasting his *CBS Melody Ranch* radio show since 1940 without any interference from Republic Pictures.

Television was a much different beast. Unlike radio an audience could remain home to "see" and hear the action.

There was another factor in the battle between film studios and television producers. The major studios where allowed to also own their own movie theaters, thus it was nothing to visit the local "Fox" or "Paramount" Theater to see a double bill they controlled. The major studios worried that not only would their films suffer from revenue loss but their movie houses as well.

Television began to hit its stride in 1948 & '49. At the same time the Supreme Court sought to forbid major film studios from distributing and exhibiting thus ceasing additional revenue through manipulative booking practices. By 1954, movie studios were forced to divest themselves of theater holdings all together. With their theater investments gone major film studios like Warner Brothers and MGM began to take advantage of TV production by 1955. But in 1949 theaters were trying every trick they could to get a full audience for each showing.

Today a multi-plex only allows a patron to see the film once before they must leave. In 1949 you could stay all day if you wanted with one low admission price and movies changed every Wednesday unless held over. Contests would be held that offered everything from dishes and refrigerators to a week with your favorite movie star.

When the studios realized they would eventually no longer have control over movie theaters they began to develop new visual forms for the screen trying to keep the people coming.

3-D had been around since the late 1800s, but it hadn't really been developed for theatrical use until 1939 for display at the New York World's Fair. 3-D was introduced to the mainstream theaters in 1952 with *Bwana Devil* starring Robert Stack and Nigel Bruce by using a dual strip film and special equipment.

That same year *This is Cinerama* premiered. Cinerama required three screens, two of them curved around the wall of the first few rows in the theater creating a feeling of being right in the action. The three projector system required three separate films to sync up to be run simultaneously. The seams between the separate films on the three screens were usually visible.

Over time the newness of both effects would become a nuisance to the audience and to the theater owners who had to install the special equipment.

The following year 20th Century Fox ushered in a much easier form of wide screen entertainment with CinemaScope. It was a practical way to present a wide screen experience with a special type of wide angel lens which would be used under different names for years to come. CinemaScope and Cinerama were the fore-runners of the IMAX system used today and easier forms of 3-D have been introduced as well, including for television.

Republic Pictures was one of the first to offer its film library to TV under the Hollywood Television Service banner. This wouldn't hurt Gene Autry who had left the studio years before, but Roy Rogers would have a tough go trying to get into television, being under contract to the studio and trying to beat them at getting his old films on television. Later, legal complications from Herbert J. Yates would cause no end to the problems. Today both Roy and Gene's backlog of Republic Pictures are owned by their respective estates.

Broncho Billy had been there at the start of the film era. Then it was Tom Mix, Ken Maynard, Buck Jones, Hoot Gibson, and Tim McCoy who ushered in sound. Now it would be

RIDING the HOLLYWOOD TRAIL II

Hoppy, Gene, Cisco, The Lone Ranger, Roy and, once again, stalwart Tim McCoy who would bring western fans into the golden era of television as they blazed the early television trail.

***

CHAPTER THREE

I'll Just Hop – A - Long

The top three stars of "B" westerns during the 1930s and '40s would always be Gene, Roy, and William Boyd. Gene was number one until he went to war. From then on, even after returning to film making, he would remain second to Roy in the polls. Boyd would continually remain in the top five, usually coming in third.

The difference between the three was that while Roy and Gene were always Roy and Gene, William Boyd would be forever known to fans through his alter ego Hopalong Cassidy. Gene and Roy also were singing cowboys, something that Boyd resisted adding for some time.

Although Boyd had been a huge matinee idol during the silent era, once he took on the "Hoppy" mantle he would never again play anything else on the silver screen. Eventually they both became one and the same on screen and off.

In 1931 a case of mistaken identity and scandal caused Boyd several lean years. Another actor by the name of William Boyd was arrested on gambling and liquor charges. Because our William Boyd was the bigger star his face was the one that appeared in the newspapers. The mistake was corrected but by that time Boyd was terminated from a studio contract he had signed the day before the scandal broke at Radio Pictures (RKO).

The whole story is covered in the first *Riding the Hollywood Trail*. This was before the Screen Actors' Guild was formed in 1933 and made it impossible for two actors to be union members with the same exact name. Because the guilty Boyd was known more for stage productions than film he would continue as William "Stage" Boyd.

The damage was done and after a few lead roles including **The Painted Desert**, billed above a young Clark Gable, and **Beyond Victory**, which also featured an unknown named Fred Scott, who would go on to have a career as a singing cowboy within a few years, our matinee idol looked like he was finished. Ironically William "Stage" Boyd would die from substance abuse in 1935, the same year the first Hopalong Cassidy film opened.

CHARLIE LeSUEUR

To show how far Bill Boyd's career had slipped, in 1935 he was offered the supporting role of Buck Peters, foreman of the Bar 20 Ranch, some accounts say a villian, in a new film called ***Hop-A-Long Cassidy***.

Supposedly he would have a featured role in support of his ***Beyond Victory*** co-star James Gleason who was going to star as Hopalong Cassidy. Gleason looked very much like the character author Clarence E. Mulford described in his stories and books as a rough talking, tobacco chewing, bow-legged, skinny little red head with a limp.

Because of a contract dispute actor Gleason backed out of the lead role and Harry 'Pop' Sherman, a very wise independent producer, was convinced to give Boyd a try as Hopalong Cassidy capitalizing on his past star status. This is the story that's been past down through the ages. The fact that Gleason signed a long term contract with RKO in August of 1935 is rarely mention in the story.

Wisely Boyd convinced Sherman to change the character in order for the series to maintain it's appeal over a series of films and the "Hoppy" we all know and love was invented. As the series went on Boyd would try different variations on the costume, but would always go back to the darker color.

In the original dark blue costume (looking black in black and white) Boyd cut quite a figure in contrast with his prematurely white hair. He successfully transformed Hopalong

Cassidy into a kinder, gentler version of Mulford's character, one that men, women and children could enjoy.

Much like Ian Fleming, at first, hated and then accepted Sean Connery's interpretation of his James Bond creation Mulford didn't like the Hollywood style interpretation of his character. Over time he would grow fonder of it as fame and monetary gratitude came his way.

With *Hop-a-Long Cassidy* aka *Hopalong Cassidy Enters* Sherman would produce 41 Cassidy films released through Paramount Pictures and another 13 through United Artists.

In the first film, *Hop-a-Long Cassidy*, the character would aptly be named Bill Cassidy. Cassidy had no limp as he did in print. To remedy this he was shot in the leg to which he said, "Oh, I'll just manage to hop along." The incident was quickly forgotten in further episodes but the nickname, "Hopalong" or "Hoppy" stuck.

For the next nine years Sherman and Boyd made a great team. In 1944, Sherman decided to discontinue the series and concentrate on bigger productions such as *Buffalo Bill* with Joel McCrea – a film it's been said was first offered to William Boyd. The actor now faced another dilemma, that of being typecast.

Rex Allen told me in an interview that he had been approached by Sherman around 1944 to appear in a series of Hoppy films but we never got around to discussing whether it was as a singing Hopalong Cassidy or possibly a young sidekick to the character.

During this time Boyd was approached by some business men to possibly be their front man in acquiring the rights to the character and continue the independent series. Through negotiations Boyd did indeed get the rights to continue filming. In 1946, after a two year hiatus, the further adventures of Hoppy continued under Hopalong Cassidy/William Boyd Productions and released through United Artists.

Compared to Sherman's Hopalong Cassidy films the new series was a bit on the cheap side. To the fans however a lower budget Hoppy was better than no Hoppy at all. Twelve more series entries were filmed between 1946 and 1948.

But the end of the silver screen Hoppy was actually just the beginning of the wealth of success Boyd would find in the next few years. Hoppy as portrayed by William Boyd had always been a good representative of morals to the younger audience members. He didn't smoke, drink and rarely got the girl – usually leaving that to his young sidekick.

In 1948, Boyd felt that there still might be life in Hoppy, not in the neighborhood theaters but in the new medium of television. By the final year of the Hoppy features, Boyd had bought all rights to the final group of films released through United Artists from his partners. He then went to Harry Sherman and arranged a deal to buy all rights to his Hopalong Cassidy film series for $350,000. The deal was made with the exception that Sherman would maintain rights to the first film *Hop-a-Long Cassidy*, which had been re-released as *Hopalong Cassidy Enters* minus the hyphens.

NBC television had been broadcasting on and off through the 1940s. In June of 1948 they had the first full-fledged television star with Milton Berle and *The Texaco Star Theatre*. With this show the network was off and running and looking for product. Boyd approached them about showing the old Cassidy films.

The following June, 1949, NBC began showing the old films, cut to fit an hour with commercials. It was a gamble for Boyd as he had used most of his money in production of the last series of films as well as buying up all rights from Sherman. The series of films were a hit and a half hour television show was ordered, thus being the first western series on TV.

Initially the final twelve features where edited to fit the half hour while Boyd developed new 30 minute episodes for television. On September 9th, 1952 the first original half hour episode aired starring Boyd and Edgar Buchanan as Red Connors, a character created by Mulford and in a few earlier films.

The new 30 minute show was popular, Boyd's now sleek black outfit was complete, but the show was not without a bit of controversy. In 1948, the Mutual Broadcasting System began to air a radio version of Hopalong Cassidy with Boyd and Andy Clyde as California Carlson from the film series. The program moved to CBS with the last radio programs recorded in August of 1951, the show would continue to be broadcast until 1952.

One year later the new 30 minute TV episodes where in production and Andy Clyde was conspicuously absent, replaced by Buchanan. It's true that while appearing on the Hopalong Cassidy radio show Clyde was doing duty as Whip Wilson's sidekick on screen but that ended in February of 1951, leaving him open for the Hoppy television show.

The film history of Andy Clyde is interesting enough to spend a few minutes on. To cover his whole career would take an entire book so let's start with his film experience.

Clyde started out in 1920 with Mack Sennett. From the start he would usually play roles older than a man in his early twenties. Clyde had the distinction of appearing or starring in more short subject comedies than any other star including The Three Stooges. From 1924 through 1956, Clyde would appear in theatrical comedy shorts while still riding the range with Hoppy and later Whip Wilson.

During those years he also kept himself busy in supporting roles in major films as well. In 1957, he gained a whole new audience of baby boomers when he began a long run on *The Real McCoys* as Walter Brennan's friend George MacMichael for 30 episodes through 1963. In 1959, he would also begin a long run as Cully Wilson on *Lassie* which ended in 1964. His last role as Jim Anderson was in 5 episodes of the short lived television version of *No Time for Sergeants* in 1964 and '65.

After appearing in nearly 400 features and shorts, Andy Clyde passed away at the relatively early age of 75 in 1967—a fact that surprised many people who thought he was much older due to the parts he played throughout his career.

As if all his other credits during the 1940s weren't enough, Clyde signed on to be the permanent replacement for George "Gabby" Hayes in the Hopalong Cassidy series in 1940. In his first film in the series, *Three Men from Texas*, Clyde was known as "California Jack" Carlson. That would be shortened to simply "California" Carlson from then on.

From 1940 through 1948, Andy rode alongside Bill Boyd and various young sidekicks for a total of 35 films in the series. As stated, during this time he continued making his short films for Columbia Pictures – the same studio that shot the Three Stooges shorts, and like the popular comedy trio (which consisted of Moe Howard, Larry Fine, and Joe Besser at the time) Andy's short films contract were terminated in 1956 when Harry Cohn, President of Columbia Pictures, decided to close the short film department.

The Hoppy film series officially ended with *Strange Gamble* in 1948. That same year a film Andy had shot in 1944 was finally released to theaters. The film *The Sundown Riders* co-starred Russell Wade and Jay Kirby as "The Sundowners," a group not unlike The Three Mesquiteers, The Range Busters, or any number of cowboy film trios—including the Hoppy series. This would be Russell Wade's final film after 80 credits to his name, usually playing a featured role. He would gain more success when he developed the El Dorado Country Club in Palm Springs holding the title of Chairman of the Palm Springs Golf Classic Tournament—now the Bob Hope Classic—for many years.

Kirby had appeared alongside Hoppy and California as Johnny Travers in six entries in the Hoppy series in 1942 and '43, just before this extremely independent film was shot on 16mm for what appears to be for school and industrial showings—possibly to get money to film other Sundowner adventures.

Andy didn't let any dust gather under his boots. By January of 1949, Hoppy's film sidekick, California Carlson, rode over to Monogram Pictures where he became "Winks" to Whip Wilson.

Obviously Andy was still playing California Carlson on radio and was forbidden from using that moniker with his Whip Wilson series, but his character name of "Winks" is interesting because he never seemed to settle on a last name. From film to film Andy was either "Winks Winkle," 'Winks Grayson,' 'Trigger Winks,'or 'Winks McGee.'

Another interesting tidbit I found while researching Andy's time with Whip is that there seems to have been two companies filming the Whip Wilson series—Monogram Pictures 1949 and '50 and Transwestern Pictures in 1950 and early '51 which were released through Monogram. These films are easy to tell apart in that the ones filmed by Transwestern Andy uses other sidekick names – Luke Watson, J. Quincey Jones, Jake Jones, 'Hungry' Rogers, and 'Sagebrush' Charlie, but never 'Winks.'

By 1950, Andy Clyde was arguably in the upper ranks of sidekicks and might have even been up there with the "Royal Three" George 'Gabby' Hayes, Smiley Burnette, and Al 'Fuzzy' St. John. He'd been riding with Hoppy in films and on radio since 1940 and would have been quite an asset to the new Hopalong Cassidy television show. So why didn't William Boyd use him?

According to Clyde, Boyd had given his word to Andy to use him in the series. Andy was disappointed that Boyd didn't keep his promise, instead signing Edgar Buchanan. Clyde didn't know about the change until he read about it in Variety. The logical reason for Boyd not to use Andy may have been that if the Whip Wilson films continued they may have kept Andy from the quick shooting pace needed for the low budget Hoppy TV series. No matter what the reason, Clyde's sidekick days came to a halt in 1952 when both the Hopalong Cassidy radio show and the Whip Wilson feature series ceased production. Boyd did realize his mistake later on and offered Clyde his role on the show but the damage was done and Andy refused.

Another puzzling matter was the exclusion of a young sidekick for Hopalong Cassidy. Throughout the film series Hoppy had a good-looking, usually hot-headed, young sidekick to bounce the scenario off of. It could have been that Boyd felt in a 30 minute program with commercials there wasn't any room for the second sidekick. Unfortunately Boyd missed one point, while kids wanted to see Hoppy they also associated with the younger action hero.

At 57, Boyd wasn't quite the gallant hero he was just a few years before and portly 49 year old Edgar Buchanan as Red Connor didn't help move the action along. Truth be told, Andy Clyde was only three years older than Boyd.

Because of the star's age, but more because of time constraint to get product out, there wasn't much action on the show, most of it taking place off screen, with Boyd's voice-over telling viewers what had happened to fill in any gaps. Boyd had originally utilized this voice-over format when he edited his features to fit the 30 minute time slot and he continued the practice with the new TV segments. It was a cheap way to make the series and, with television in its infancy, still hold the viewer's fascination. Unfortunately the TV show doesn't hold up today as well as some of its contemporaries like the Cisco Kid or Gene Autry.

Buchanan would be put to better use by Russell Hayden's production company when he was cast in syndication as *Judge Roy Bean* for 39 episodes in 1955-56.

Still for it's time the Hopalong Cassidy TV show was a ground-breaking program. Boyd or should we say Hopalong Cassidy was featured on the cover of Look, Time, and Life magazines, something brand new for the former star of a "B" western series. Furthermore, Boyd was the first TV star to see the full potential of merchandising, earning nearly one million dollars in 1950 alone.

In May of 1951, Boyd invested in Hoppyland, a Venice, California amusement park which was renamed after he became an investor. This may have been considered the only loss in the Hoppy dynasty as it closed in 1954—the next year Disneyland would open in nearby Anaheim. Today the Hoppyland location is part of Marina del Rey.

In 1952, Hoppy would make one last appearance on the silver screen and in color. William Boyd became a star when Cecil B. DeMille starred him in *The Volga Boatman* (1926). It had been 25 years since Boyd had last appeared for DeMille in the original *King of Kings* (1927) when he was asked to appear in *The Greatest Show on Earth* as Hoppy. It was an indication that William Boyd had come full circle and was being recognized by the great director as an icon of film and television.

Since his death, his company still oversees Hopalong Cassidy merchandise including the lucrative video business. He has a star on the Hollywood Walk of Fame and probably more importantly he was inducted posthumously into the Western Hall of Fame at the National Cowboy & Western Heritage Museum in Oklahoma City. Finally, every year the Hopalong Cassidy Festival is held in Cambridge, Ohio near Boyd's hometown of Belmont. Just like Roy is Roy and Gene is Gene, William Boyd is Hoppy, and from where he is looking down upon us—he is proud of it. Can't you just hear that familiar laugh?

***

CHAPTER FOUR

We Gotta Get a Bigger Mask

Arguably, no western hero has been more mishandled over the years than the Lone Ranger. Unlike Batman, Spider-Man, or any other masked hero, the masked man of the west is definitely a product of his time, not only in the old west, but on early radio, film, and television.

With today's savvy audience it's extremely hard to convey the excitement baby-boomers felt each week watching Clayton Moore and Jay Silverheels in their latest adventure.

Whereas other masked heroes can be dusted off and updated to the 21st century, The Lone Ranger must remain in the 1800s west. And for today's young audience to accept the premise it must be done a bit tongue in cheek. This along with the fact that

Tonto just isn't politically correct makes it difficult to give the Lone Ranger a decent pulpit.

Witness the last effort by Johnny Depp as Tonto, which on paper seemed to work. The film itself isn't bad–taken in the right context it's actually quite fun, pure escapism–but who is its audience?

The problem with the film is that its target audience, those between early teens to thirty-five, couldn't relate and many baby boomers who feel very protective about the characters didn't like the way the subject was treated.

The mask, the powder blue stretch-pants, and the faithful Indian companion—not to mention that 'Kemo Sabe' still up for debate as to what Tonto was really calling the Lone Ranger—are all, unfortunately, irrelevant today.

It's not that the Ranger hasn't failed before on the big and small screen – Klinton Spilsbury anyone? Yes, the 1981 film was a mistake on so many levels, but what about the 2003 TV film that changed the character in order to make it palatable for the ***Beverly Hills 90210*** crowd? It failed to do well enough to make a proposed TV series.

The official premiere episode of ***The Lone Ranger*** debuted on WXYZ in Detroit, Michigan on January 30th, 1933. However there is significant proof to show that Fran Striker created the character for Buffalo station WEBR prior to the official premiere. It was during these local Buffalo broadcasts that

George W.Trendle, station owner of WXYZ in Detroit, talked Striker into coming over to the much larger Detroit market.

With this move the character becomes shrouded in a bit of controversy. Both station owner George W. Trendle and main writer Fran Striker take credit for actually coming up with the exact concept. Although Striker had already used basic concepts of the series earlier for *Covered Wagon Days* and initial Buffalo broadcasts, Trendle took credit for creating the character specifically for WXYZ.

Studying the origin further may show that there were other inspirations for the character. John Reynolds Hughes was a Texas Ranger active from 1887 to early 1915. Events that support this theory include his hunt for the killers responsible for the ambush of Texas Ranger Captain Frank Jones and his later assignment to protect a silver mine. In the hunt for Captain Jones killers the record shows that eighteen were caught and either shot or hung. A silver mine comes into play with the origin of the Lone Ranger.

Hughes was also the subject of many books including Zane Grey's *The Lone Star Ranger* which was first made into a film in 1919 with William Farnum, then 1923 with Tom Mix, 1930 with George O' Brien and again in 1942 with Texas A & M football star John Kimbrough.

To his unfortunate death by suicide in 1947 at the age of 92, Hughes insisted that he was the inspiration for the Lone Ranger. But in the last few years there's been a debate over this claim.

Recently, it's been pointed out that Striker and Trendle may have embellished on the character's origins by using a local Detroit legend. Bass Reeves was a former slave turned lawman who served as a Deputy US Marshal for thirty-two years at the turn of the 20th century.

Although his story takes place during a different time period in a different area, Oklahoma and Western Arkansas, the similarities cannot be denied. Further proof is the surname of the Lone Ranger being Reid is very close to Reeves. Okay, a bit of a stretch you might say? How about this, very often the Marshals were accompanied by Native Americans. In Reeves case it was said to be a Potawatomi.

More proof can also be found in a "silver" connection. While The Lone Ranger was known for using silver bullets, Reeves was said to use a silver dollar as a calling card.

His horse was described as a "large grey." Adult greys have a white coat. Further strong proof is that Reeves would often use disguises when tracking the bad guys, just like The Lone Ranger.

Bass Reeves was a fearless and ambidextrous crack shot with either hand who captured 3,000 criminals, killed 14 men who wouldn't give up, and brought in 17 bad guys by himself during one round-up—plus he was never wounded.

In the Detroit area, where a large number of the criminals that Bass Reeves captured over his career were sent to federal prison, he had songs written and stories told about his many exploits. A low budget direct to video film was even made in 2010, and there has been interest expressed in a big budget film based on his life. So why is this great lawman not celebrated like Wyatt Earp and Pat Garrett. Upon reading about his exploits it could be argued very easily that he has a history that would put Earp and Garrett to shame.

It's very possible that once Striker brought his Buffalo, New York ideas to Detroit, Michigan, Trendle added much of the legendary stories and lore about Bass Reeves. Of course back then a black hero on radio would never do. Originally, in print, a black mask completely covered The Lone Ranger's face, which only later was trimmed down. Was this a nod to Bass Reeves?

In 1934, Trendle pressured Striker to sign over all rights to The Lone Ranger. Its true Trendle did own the character. Because it takes both the venue and the writer to bring a program to success, I'm going to sit on the fence with this one and say they both helped to make The Lone Ranger the character fans love.

Trendle may have been the one to fashion the character in the form of Bass Reeves, I will absolutely give him credit for that. So while Striker had the basic idea in Buffalo, it wasn't until The Lone Ranger's premiered in Detroit that the premise truly was formed into the character we know as The Lone Ranger. Because of this I can see the split in sides.

In the future, however, it would be Stiker who would indeed have the most far reaching influence on the Ranger for comic strips, two movie serials, novels and the TV series that would far outlast anything Trendle brought to the character.

The first film incarnation came in 1938 with the fifteen chapter serial *The Lone Ranger* for Republic Pictures. The film unfolds as a mystery. While indeed rangers are led into an ambush it's unclear as to who remains to become The Lone Ranger until the last chapter—spoiler alert, it's Lee Powell as Allen King.

The changes to the familiar storyline upset Trendle but he didn't have much say in the matter. No less than six writers were attributed to writing the script with Striker being given writing credit, obviously because of his help in the character's original creation.

Trendle had signed an ironclad contract with Herbert J. Yates of Republic Pictures saying the studio could do what they wished with the property. The studio was known for making the best quality serials at the time—they were also known for altering the stories and characters at their whim, possibly the worst being their treatment of *Captain America* with Lee Powell.

Even though Trendle was upset, it didn't stop him from cashing the checks he received for Republic's use of the character. Republic Pictures contract also gave them permission to release a feature version of the serial which they did in 1940 as *Hi-Yo Silver*.

Keep in mind that the radio show was only 6 years old so tinkering with the origins of the Lone Ranger was nothing that Republic felt they needed to concern themselves with. The character being 'John' Reid hadn't been set either – many today still maintain that Dan Reid is the Lone Ranger or that he doesn't have a first name, which makes him more mysterious. The name "John" wouldn't be uttered on film until 1981's ***The Legend of the Lone Ranger***.

Republic Pictures first Lone Ranger serial was a huge success and negotiations for a sequel of sorts were arranged in the summer of 1938 as ***The Lone Ranger Returns***. Lee Powell was asked to reprise the role plus a term contract with Republic—Powell's agent asked for too much money and so Lee was left out when the title was changed to ***The Lone Ranger Rides Again*** for a 1939 release.

This time the Ranger was played by the very popular cowboy star, Robert Livingston of Three Mesquiteers fame. The Ranger was given a new secret identity as Bill Andrews to avoid any identification with Lee Powell's Allen King—however Chief Thundercloud (Victor Daniels) was again to play Tonto.

Because Livingston had a tremendous fan base in "B" westerns this outing was a straight-forward action story. No mystery as to who The Lone Ranger actually was gave Livingston reason to spend much of his screen time minus the mask—much like 20th Century Fox did when Tyrone Power played Zorro for them in ***The Mark of Zorro*** the following year.

A film version was never made of *The Lone Ranger Rides Again*.

Even though both serials had been a tremendous success and furthered the fame for the Lone Ranger, Trendle was agitated by Republic's tampering with his "creation" not once but twice. He decided to peddle the character elsewhere.

He approached Universal Pictures but nothing came of the negotiations. Universal would, however, release two serials based on The Green Hornet. The character of Britt Reid a.k.a. The Green Hornet was another creation by Trendle and Striker and was originally given a relationship to The Lone Ranger by making his father Dan Reid, the Ranger's nephew.

In the TV show Dan Reid would be played by Chuck Courtney for 14 episodes. This would primarily be used to help ease the load on Jay Silverheels who suffered ill health throughout the run of the show. As time went on and decade upon decade spaced the time period of The Lone Ranger from that of each version of The Green Hornet the relationship had to be separated even further. Eventually this relationship would be played down. The link is still there as far as their respective musical themes being classical pieces - The Lone Ranger's being Rossini's *William Tell Overture* and The Green Hornet's being Rimsky-Korsakov's *Flight of the Bumblebee*.

From here the story of both serials becomes a bit murky. Either Trendle eventually gained rights to both serials and the

35mm negatives were destroyed on purpose or they were misplaced by Republic Pictures and possibly destroyed because of nitrate decomposition.

Both serials were considered lost for many years. Copies of both serials were found in Mexico and Europe and hastily pieced using stills and awkward exposition to fill gaps. Various forms were available from multiple dealers. These were of inferior quality because of the prints and equipment available at the time. For example, *The Lone Ranger Rides Again* was only available in English with Spanish subtitles.

Today, through the latest technology, both serials have been fully restored minus subtitles using the best quality in video and audio available. As of this writing, The Serial Squadron is the only company to order your copies from to be sure of getting this quality.

The Lone Ranger had been successful on radio and with altered serial versions but the version that we grew to know and love came with the inspired casting of Clayton Moore and Jay Silverheels as the Lone Ranger and Tonto.

The television show is basically the template for everything that followed. Like George Reeves will always be Superman to Baby Boomers, Clayton Moore will be the Lone Ranger no matter who puts on the mask.

While June of 1949 saw the premiere of heavily edited versions of Hopalong Cassidy films on TV, the honors for the first expressly made for television western series belongs to *The Lone Ranger* in September of that year.

Today, TV western fans take for granted that Clayton Moore is and always will be the Lone Ranger. In 1949, he was just another actor making a living in "B" films and serials. As a matter of fact, even after signing on to wear the mask he would continue to appear in other films and TV shows, sometimes unbilled, including one episode of *Hopalong Cassidy*, two episodes of *The Range Rider*, one episode of *Annie Oakley* and three episodes of *The Gene Autry Show*.

Granted some were done while John Hart had replaced him as the Ranger, but not all – perhaps he wanted to make sure he kept working in case he was fired again. Whatever role he took there was no mistaking his distinctive voice, something *The Lone Ranger* producers would take for granted when trying to replace him. Once Clayton Moore appeared as the Ranger no other would do.

For the TV version Trendle hired veteran MGM producer Jack Chertok. Chertok would also produce *Sky King*, *Steve Donovan - Western Marshal*, and *The Lawless Years*. In his later career he would be the executive producer for *My Favorite Martian*.

By the time the television show premiered most of the original origin story was in place. Butch Cavendish and his gang ambush the rangers leaving only Dan Reid's younger brother to avenge their deaths and become the "Lone" Ranger. The origin would be tweaked from time to time—especially the Ranger's relationship with Tonto, but the underlying story has remained the same. The television show is basically the template for everything that followed.

On radio *The Lone Ranger* had been played by several actors. The actor most associated with the character is Brace Beemer who voiced the character from 1941 until the end of the radio show in 1954.

Originally George (Stenius) Seaton voiced the Ranger briefly from January 31, to May 9th, 1933. Earle Graser had already been chosen to take over the role when Seaton left. Graser would continue in the role until his tragic death in an automobile accident on April 8th, 1941.

Brace had been doing the famous "Hi-Yo Silver, Away" almost from the beginning as well as appearing as the Lone Ranger for public appearances due to his commanding appearance, so it was a natural for him to completely take the reins after Graser's death. He would continue to voice the famous line throughout the run of the TV series, when it was decided that he was not much of an actor to play the part on camera. Moore would even attempt to pattern his speech after Beemer's in the early episodes.

In the beginning actor Gerald Mohr would do the narration for the first 16 episodes of the television version and then Fred Foy—who had been the narrator and announcer for the radio version—was retained as announcer until the end of its run.

Today it's hard to imagine a series running for 78 new continuous episodes before taking a break, but that's exactly what was done for the TV series. These original 78 would air twice before new episodes began. This means that these episodes ran for two full years before the Hart episodes began.

When new episodes began for the third season in 1952 with *The Outlaw's Son* (September 11th, 1952) something was different. Although production had ceased long before the second run of the original 78 episodes, the show had been consistently on the tube. However, when the Lone Ranger returned with Jay Silverheels as Tonto something was different about the Ranger. What happened? Certainly Clayton Moore was never seen without the mask unless he was in disguise to foil some dastardly deed. But fans couldn't be fooled—this was not The Lone Ranger they knew and loved.

Supposedly John Hart was signed to play the part after Moore asked for more money. In his autobiography, *I Was That Masked Man*, Moore denies the notion that the split was over money. What he does say is that Trendle intended to replace him at least a year prior to his firing.

One reason Clayton Moore gives for his dismissal is that Trendle was very possessive of the Ranger—he did indeed take full advantage on the end credits of being the creator of the character. According to Moore, he felt Trendle didn't like anyone else being associated with the character in the minds of the public.

It does sound feasible. Moore had been toiling in the ranks of grade 'B' supporting actors for so long, and the TV show was still in its infancy. It seems almost unfeasible for him to have asked for more money so quickly. But the story does persist that this is exactly why he was let go.

Moore's reasoning for his belief that Trendle was planning on firing him at least a year before the dismissal is that the producer ordered the Ranger's mask made larger to cover most of his face. If this is true then the trouble would have started much earlier in the first season. In studying the episodes it's clear that The Lone Ranger began to wear the larger mask in episode 7 of season one, *Pete and Pedro*. This means the original 'smaller' mask only lasted for six episodes before the change. If there was a dispute over money surely it would have been brought up when it came time to renegotiate Moore's contract and not so early in the first season?

The mask became even bigger when John Hart took over for the third season and the next fifty-two entries—it still couldn't hide the fact that this was not The Lone Ranger people had been used to watching for two years.

The audience couldn't be fooled by the replacement and ratings eventually began to plummet. It probably didn't help that while first run episodes with Hart were airing on ABC, reruns with Moore were being shown Saturday mornings on CBS. If Trendle wanted to erase the memory of Clayton Moore as The Lone Ranger he wasn't doing a very good job of it.

In addition the first three episodes from 1949, explaining how The Lone Ranger came to be, were edited together by Trendle as *The Legend of the Lone Ranger* in 1952 and released theatrically. With Clayton Moore still highly visible as the masked man John Hart didn't have a chance.

It's clear that the show's opening with Clayton Moore riding Silver was never changed to feature Hart, while episode budgets were definitely cut to eliminate location shooting in favor of more sound stage bound sets.

It's hard to imagine that for exactly one year, *The Lone Ranger* was 'Mooreless.' With *The Fugitive,* season four, episode 1 (September 9th 1954) Moore returned without any fanfare. Moore says he doesn't know why he was re-hired—ratings maybe? Another theory is that Trendle was preparing to sell the property to another producer and felt that Moore would help raise the ante in the sell.

However the mask remained as large as it had with John Hart. Maybe the producers figured the audience could be fooled into thinking it had been Clayton Moore all along...hmmm, I don't think so—not with Moore's repeats being run against Hart's episodes.

It would appear that season four may have been a restart with Clayton in that not much changed in production values from the previous season with John Hart. The season consisted of another fifty-two new episodes.

The next year and season five changed all that. George Trendle sold the rights to producer Jack Wrather. Wrather had made his money in oil before he entered television production and a major change showed on screen.

At the time of his purchase Wrather had been married to actress Bonita Granville for seven years. Best known for her role in the *Nancy Drew* film series of the 1930s - she would go on to oversee television production of *Lassie* as well as other Wrather productions.

Jack Wrather brought a gloss to *The Lone Ranger*. The final season of first run episodes were shot in color with the usual 39 episodes—the amount normal for first run shows at the time—and yes, the mask got much smaller. There was less studio bound shooting and more use of natural locations to enhance the scope of this final season and give it a more mature feeling.

The final first run episode was *Outlaws in Greasepaint* (June 6th, 1957) which featured my good friend, Mary Ellen Kay(e). Before Trendle released the Ranger to Wrather he did reshoot the origin for a 1955 tele-film *The Lone Ranger Rides Again* – not to be confused with the earlier Republic Pictures serial. Glenn Strange – the ultimate Butch Cavendish - returned to reprise the role. This film was made to commemorate the 22nd anniversary of the Lone Ranger's creation and possibly to let Trendle toot his own horn one last time. Some contend the film is non-existant, but having a copy myself I can tell you it does indeed exist.

The very next year, Wrather produced a big budget color feature film for Warner Bro., *The Lone Ranger.* To date this is the very best example of the Ranger and Tonto on the big screen. Not to mention that it was made by a major studio. This was a more adult approached to the subject matter and shows that a film utilizing these characters could be made that appeals to adults as much as the younger crowd. Co-producer Bonita Granville made a film appearance as Lyle Bettger's wife, "Welcome Kilgore." The film utilized various familiar locations in the L.A. area such as Iverson Ranch, Warner Ranch and the familiar Bronson Caves. The production also made good use of the Kanab Movie Ranch and other locations around Southern Utah.

Wrather produced another feature *The Lone Ranger and the Lost City of Gold* in 1958. While it was good to see Moore and Silverheels together one more time on the big screen it doesn't match up to the previous motion picture and falls more in line with the TV show. The film did benefit from location shooting at Old Tucson. Instead of Warner Bros. this film was released by United Artists.

In all Moore would play the Lone Ranger in 169 episodes, two feature films, *The Lone Ranger*(1956) and *The Lone Ranger and the Lost City of Gold(* 1958) plus one compilation film from edited TV episodes, *The Legend of the Lone Ranger*

(1952) and the 22nd Anniversary telefilm ***The Lone Ranger Rides Again*** (1955).

Moore and Silverheels would return to their characters in TV commercials such as Stan Freberg's highly entertaining commercial for Jeno's Pizza Rolls in the 1960s and in the 1970s to advertise Aqua Velva After Shave. In 1986 Tostitos used vintage footage of the Lone Ranger and Tonto from the TV series to cleverly edit a commercial intertwined with a new character. This is why it's in black and white and Moore is once again wearing the larger mask—not to mention Silverheels passed away in 1980. With an ingenious 1981 Sun Sensor Lenses commercial, Moore would make fun of the frivolous lawsuit filed by the Wrather Corporation to stop him from appearing in the mask. In 1988—restored to full Lone Ranger Status and in great shape—74 year old Moore appeared in an Amoco Gas commercial. All these commercials can be found on YouTube.

Hart, however, wasn't done with the character. He would play the Lone Ranger on one episode of ***The Greatest American Hero*** in 1981 and the following year on ***Happy Days***, still looking very fit in the costume. Also, in 1981, he played Lucas Striker—in tribute to Lone Ranger co-creator Fran Striker—in the ill-fated feature film ***The Legend of the Lone Ranger*** starring Klinton Spilsbury. There's no mention of anyone named Trendle. It would be Spilsbury's only feature film to date. The only possible name link in the 2013 film is a character named Clayton.

One more mention of the 1981 film, *The Legend of the Lone Ranger* should be made and then we can forget it. The main weakness of the film is the lead actor, Klinton Spilsbury. No actor has ever had such a fall from grace—even George Lazenby as James Bond—than poor Mr. Spilsbury. Not only was he unsuited for the role, lacking any charisma, but his dialogue had to be redubbed by actor James Keach.

It didn't help matters any that the producers of this film had a court injunction filed against Clayton Moore to prevent him from appearing in public wearing a mask. Moore had never denied his days as the Lone Ranger, far from it. It would be a rare occasion when he would make a public appearance without the mask until the court order. After that he would wear stylized sunglasses to give himself the appearance of the traditional mask hence the Sun Sensor Lenses commercial in 1981.

Because of the producer's refusal to recognize Clayton Moore's place in the Ranger's history, fans ignored the film. Others who had grown up without the Lone Ranger couldn't identify with the character. Put the two together and it spelled disaster for the film and the one in 2013.

A rather obscure pilot called *The Return of the Lone Ranger* was supposedly shot in 1961 starring stuntman/actor Tex Hill. I did have a conversation with Tex, a very amiable gentleman, in the early 1990s. He would wear the Lone Ranger outfit and sell his self-produced video westerns at festivals. The pilot is listed in both his and Trendle's IMDb site. Tex passed away on February 28th 2014 in Wickenburg, Arizona.

Television did try to revive the character in 2003 with a totally forgettable WB network telefilm, *The Lone Ranger*. Starring teen heartthrob Chad Michael Murray as "Luke Hartman" aka The Lone Ranger, the producers tried to lure the *Beverly Hills 90210* crowd to the character.

The origin remained pretty much the same although a subplot involving a possible romance between Luke and Tonto's sister, Alope, was added. *I was a Teenage Lone Ranger,* I mean this version of *The Lone Ranger* didn't catch on and the proposed TV series was shelved.

Of course the 2013 film starring Johnny Depp as Tonto with second-billed Armie Hammer as our hero surprisingly flopped at the box-office despite a winning team-up with Depp's *Pirates of the Caribbean* collaborators. It will no doubt clean- up on video, dish and cable, but a theatrical sequel is doubtful. It just may be that while pirates are very popular with the young audience of today a frontier "superhero" of sorts just doesn't appeal to them.

No matter how many times Hollywood has tried to recycle The Lone Ranger it hasn't worked. Is that a bad thing? In some way it's sad that the younger generations haven't taken to the character in new incarnations. Western heroes don't have the same draw as pirates and space cadets to the video game audience of today.

Classical music lovers however, no matter how devoted, have to admit with possible irritation that Rossini's *William Tell Overture* will always be better known as *The Lone Ranger Theme* and film and television fans will always have to admit that no matter who plays the masked man, Clayton Moore will always be, The Loooone Ranger!

***

CHAPTER FIVE

CHAMPION Is Not Just His Horse

Gene Autry is indeed a prize Champion. He may not have been the best looking, the tallest, or the best singer of the bunch, but he was a great marketer. And the thing he marketed the best was . . . Gene Autry – a Champion.

Gene Autry may not have been the first western star to make the move to television, but he is without a doubt the most successful – a Champion. Get the picture?

However, it wasn't without a bit of a struggle to free himself from the claws of Republic Studios president, Herbert J. Yates – but there was never a doubt who would win.

Gene had left his successful film career behind in 1942, becoming a tech sergeant in the Army Air Corps. It was during this time that he slipped as the top cowboy star to second place in favor of Roy Rogers.

When he returned from the war he didn't want to continue the same type of films he had left behind for Republic Pictures and told Yates he wouldn't be coming back.

The problem, as Yates pointed out, was that Gene owed the studio five more films on his pre-enlistment contract. Gene agreed to finish out the contract before he started up his own production company. Yates wouldn't make it easy for the returning veteran and it showed when he assigned character actor Sterling Holloway as his so-called sidekick for the final series.

Smiley Burnette had left Republic Pictures by 1946 and signed with Columbia Pictures where he became the sidekick to Charles Starrett's "Durango Kid" character. Due to Republic owning the rights to his "Frog Millhouse" character Smiley would finish out his "B" film career by simply using his stage name.

Sterling Holloway had been a fixture in Hollywood since 1926. His thick bushy hair made him a recognizable commodity, but it's his voice that would bring him his most fame. Becoming a regular on radio and animated Disney films he would become world famous as the voice of Winnie the Pooh. Shortly before his death he was honored by becoming a "Disney Legend," the first in the voice category.

Holloway was likable enough in any role he played, but he was drastically out of place as 2nd banana to Gene. Herbert J. Yates might have been forgiven for giving our hero such a weak side- kick if he didn't do the same thing to Roy Rogers when he decided to leave the studio. More on that later.

Starting with *Sioux City Sue* released in November of 1946, Holloway would more or less be the comedy relief through the remaining four films ending in July of 1947 with *Robin Hood of Texas*. A mere nine months and five mediocre films might have made Yates think he sunk Gene's film career. He would be wrong.

Before Gene had completed the final Republic series he had already made a deal with Columbia Pictures to head up his own independent film company. As a final act before leaving Mr. Yates in the dust he hired much of his Republic Pictures film crew and took them with him.

Without missing a beat Gene had his first production, *The Last Round-up,* in theaters by November of 1947 just four months after his last one for Republic. The tone for those to follow was set immediately. Gone were any overblown production numbers. Instead the songs would usually be an integral part of the films without being intrusive. The mood would be more somber, humor put in its place. Gene's character would be more in line with a rugged cowboy hero usually wearing jeans in place of flamboyant costumes. It fit well and today the Columbia films hold up better than his films for Republic.

With both Gene and Smiley Burnette now at Columbia you might have thought they would pair up once again. It was not to be, at least not for a while. A young comic Gene had met while working in Chicago on *The Old Barn Dance* program for WLS would have a role in his second film in the series, *The Strawberry Roan*. He wasn't Gene's sidekick yet, but after five more films Pat Buttrum was signed as Gene's permanent sidekick.

Although he basically played the same character, Pat never used the same name twice in the films until he started simply going by Pat Buttram in the films and on the TV show. Pat would later explain how this eventually happened. "Gene had a hard time remembering the different names for me in every picture and on the TV show which we were doing two or three a week, and it got confusing. Gene finally said, 'Call him Pat Buttrum.'"

In July of 1950, the same month as Gene's 13th film for Columbia, *Beyond the Purple Hills*, was released to theaters he began *The Gene Autry Show* on CBS television. Virtually everything was the same on this 30 minute program as his features including the production values. Using the same crew and topnotch western directors each show holds up very well even today.

The best thing for Gene was that Columbia Pictures didn't own any portion of his TV production company, Flying A. However, Columbia would in part profit from the TV show in that Gene turned each episode into a 30 minute commercial for his features until he ceased his film output in 1953.

Each week at the end of the TV show the announcer would proudly announce, "Be sure and see Gene and Champion in their latest full length feature at your local theater." This helped appease theater owners who might have felt Gene was betraying them by moving into television. They loved the idea that their new Gene Autry movie was being touted each week on television. It made it a winning situation for both Gene, Columbia Pictures, and the neighborhood movie theater.

To further alleviate any worry from theater owners Gene and CBS Television issued the following press release:

Speaking of Television… July 7, 1950

By GENE AUTRY

(Star of CBS-TV's "Gene Autry Show," starting Sunday, July 23)

To paraphrase a famous question, "TV or not TV" as the big problem facing me early this year. Like everyone else in show business, I had become very much interested in the possibilities of television. And, in addition, I had a special reason for wanting to hit the video channels. During my three and a half years in the service, a whole new generation of children had been born. These youngsters are still too young to attend many movies (if at all), but they're not too young to watch television. And in these days, cowboy fans, like charity, begin at home. On the other hand, Hollywood has been mighty good to me for many years and, rightly or wrongly, Hollywood considers television a threat to its own business. This is particularly true of theatre exhibitors, the men and women who own and manage the movie houses where pictures are shown. So if I did go in for television, theatre men might consider this a definite affront, an evidence of disloyalty.

Well, the problem plagued me for a good many months, but finally I reached a decision: to go ahead and produce a series of western films for CBS television. I didn't want to make my TV debut in old serials of old movies in which I had appeared 10 or 15 years ago, so I made plans to star in a brand new series of half-hour movies especially designed for the needs and limits of television. And the reasons I decided to go ahead with this venture were:

(1) most of my movies play in small towns, whereas television sets are most numerous (per capita) in the large cities; thus, these areas of competition would not overlap to any considerable extent;

(2) and more important, television can and will serve as a boon to movie business. Children, and adults, too, who see a certain star on television become interested in him and, as a result, will also go to see his movies . . . or his rodeos, or his night club act. It has worked that way in every other phase of

the entertainment business. Stardom on radio, records, or movies immediately stirs up interest in that personality in other mediums – and it is also going to be true of television. I firmly believe that.

As I write this, we have just completed the first six of our television features. They will be released for viewing on CBS television channels about the middle of July. The first one is titled "Gold Dust Charlie."

Those of you who are familiar with my CBS radio show, "Melody Ranch," will recognize quite a few of the characters in these movies as recruits from radio. In addition to myself, there's Pat (The Beard) Buttram (he calls me "the Pinza of the Plains"); Johnny Bond, who plays guitar and also acts as my "saddle pal" in the short dramatic sketches on our radio show; and the Cass County Boys, that very fine vocal and instrumental trio from out Texas way. In the feminine leads, you'll see some of my movie heroines, among them lovely Sheila Ryan. And of course Champion, the smartest horse in the movies, is co-starred.

We hope you'll like these television movies. The boys in the trade tell me they're just about the most expensive films yet made for TV. We shot them on location at Pioneertown, California, where many of my movies are filmed. Armand Schaefer, who produces my movies, has worked hard to achieve the right blend of story, action, and music in these video films. Now we'd like your reaction. Let us hear from you, won't you?

CHARLIE LeSUEUR

We plan to make about 40 more tv pictures within the next year, and we'd like to get your ideas on the subject.

* * *

Notice that first off he makes mention of his three and a half years serving the country, never a bad place to start in the time right after the war. He specifically calls his TV episodes "features" or "television movies," anything but a TV show to associate with theatre owners.

He also makes mention of not wanting to make his television debut through his old movies. This could have easily worked against him, however it was also a way to beat Republic Pictures at selling his older films to television. At first Herbert J. Yates, as with other studio heads, felt betrayed by any stars that moved to television. Over time they begrudgingly recognized that the small screen could be another stream of revenue.

To make a closer relationship with the theatrical releases, Gene and Pat would appear in a variety of locations and situations, never bound to any specific town or area. This would provide more plotlines and more characters. Gene also recognized the fact that films shot for television needed to be lensed a bit differently. By studying how films needed to be shot using 35mm film for TV he was able to tailor each scene for the new medium.

Gene studied film to the point where he noticed that stark blacks and sharp whites don't come over on the small screen so the more grays or in-between contrast shades the better.

"It's a mistake to waste much film on long shots," Gene would say. *"A medium shot is better than a long shot and a close shot is better than either."* An eye on budget while producing a glossy product is what made Gene such a sharp businessperson.

His study of the transition from the silver screen to television also moved into plot for the sake of budget. For example, keeping violence to a minimum was not necessarily to make his programs family friendly but to keep costs down. *"If the hero shoots and kills the villian, the villian gets paid extra for falling down, because he falls in the category of a stuntman. However if the hero just wounds him, there's no extra pay."* Concerning the order of a kill, *"If you kill off too many people in the first part of your story, that means you have to have a larger cast in order to finish the twenty-six minutes. So if we do kill somebody, we try to do the killing at the very end and limit it to one or two people at the most."* Even killing had a pecking order in early television.

Gene went further in his philosophy as far as script and editing. *"Keep it simple, keep it moving, keep it close and make it fast. Use simple plot lines with a minimum of counter plot."*

Each episode also had new musical cues, unlike other shows at the time that simply used "canned" music. Later most westerns in the 1950s and '60s would construct a new score each week to fit each episode.

The show was not without incident due to the quick shooting schedule. Buttram had sought out comic master Buster Keaton to school him in the art of comical stunts. He was a fast learner and it helped save time and money that he would do many of own stunts on the show. However an accident during the first season would sideline Buttram for a few episodes. While using an antique cannon Buttram was hurt during an explosion causing injury to his chest, stomach, and almost causing him to lose a foot. For much of the season he would be replaced by Alan Hale, Jr., Chill Wills and Fuzzy Knight during his recuperation.

It was easy to duplicate some previously filmed long shots of Buttram with new footage of Wills and Knight wearing Pat's costume. It was a bit more difficult in the first two replacement episodes with Hale who was much larger. Ironically, Hale was nicknamed "Tiny" in these shows. Knight would return for the first two episodes of the second season due to the fast paced shooting schedule. By then Pat was back at it.

During this recuperation time it might have occurred to some that Gene should use his old pal Smiley Burnette to fill in but it didn't happen. Perhaps to avoid confusion Gene chose not to use him – or to avoid timely costs in matching up footage with Pat Buttrum. However, Smiley did substitute for Pat in the film being shot at the time, *Whirlwind*, which was released in 1951. After that Smiley returned to the Durango Kid film series through 1952.

Two episodes in the first season, *The Raiders* and *Double Barreled Vengeance* were shot in color to promote a color process for CBS, the process wasn't found acceptable by the FCC and so the show wouldn't switch completely to color until the final season of the show in 1955.

Gene would go on to successfully produce several western TV series in the early 1950s under his Flying "A" Banner– *Annie Oakley*, *The Range Rider*, *Buffalo Bill, Jr.*, and even *Champion* rode the range in his own short lived TV series before Gene turned his attention to other lucrative endeavors such as a baseball league, The Anaheim Angels, as well as radio and television stations to mention a few of his investments.

In 1956, *The Gene Autry Show* as well as his other TV productions became a staple of Saturday mornings where many more children, the "Baby Boomers," discovered him not realizing he had been a star for over 20 years before.

***

CHAPTER SIX

White Washing the
Robin Hood of the Old West

"Here's adventure! Here's romance! Here's O. Henry's famous Robin Hood of the old west – The Cisco Kid!" Thus would start each television episode of **The Cisco Kid**.

Whitewashing the Robin Hood of the Old West had been in progress for nearly twenty years by the time the big switch to television came. In just two decades there had been 26 films and four Cisco's on the big screen—take that James Bond!

No matter which of the four actors played Cisco, the film titles were interchangeable in the series; Here's just a sample of what I mean; **The Daring Caballero**, **The Gay Caballero**, **The Gay Cavalier**, **The Gay Amigo**, **Return of the Cisco Kid**, **The**

Cisco Kid Returns, ***Romance on the Rio Grande***, ***South of the Rio Grande***. So we can tell that The Cisco Kid was a daring caballero, he loved to return by way of the Rio Grande and that he was…well…gay—meaning he was 'happy' in the vernacular of that period.

Considering the rough edged ethnic roguishness of the character it might have seemed like a daring move translating him to the early days of the small screen.

Unlike Hoppy, who was always represented by All American Bill Boyd, the Latin Cisco Kid would go through many changes of character depending on who played him. Warner Baxter, Cesar Romero, Gilbert Roland, and Duncan Renaldo would all paint Cisco with a different brush.

Surprisingly, non-Latin actor Baxter may have been the closet to O. Henry's original character, but even he was toned down to appeal to theater goers. Just read some of Cisco's characteristics as written by O. Henry and you can see how sanitized the screen version became. *"The Cisco Kid had killed six men in more or less fair scrimmages, had murdered twice as many (mostly Mexicans), and had winged a larger number whom he modestly forbore to count."*

Thus starts ***The Caballero's Way*** by O. Henry. Later on the author explains the evil motivations behind Cisco's avid use of the gun. *"He killed for the love of it—because he was quick tempered - to avoid arrest—for his own amusement – any reason that came to mind would suffice."*

Cisco's appearance was also drastically different from those who played him on screen. *"The Kid was twenty-five, looked twenty."*

Not quite the character you may remember from the TV show. Moreover he isn't even of Hispanic origin. Early in the story one character is quoted as saying: *"This hombre they call the Kid...Goodall is his name ain't it ?"*

Through O. Henry's more clever writing we learn much more about Cisco as the story evolves. *"The Kid was a vain person."*

O. Henry uses Cisco's love interest, Tonia, in describing more about the him. *"The men she had known had been short and dark. Even the Kid, in spite of his achievements, was a stripling no larger than herself."*

Through these passages we learn that the Cisco Kid was a killer, young looking, not of Hispanic origin, arrogant and short in stature. Not what we are used to seeing on the big or small screen.

In the first film version of **The Caballero's Way** in 1914 the character remained more or less as it was in the short story. Cisco would return to the silent screen in 1919 in **Border Terror**. By the time Fox Film Corporation made a semi-remake of **The Caballero's Way**, called **In Old Arizona** (1928), Cisco became just a bit more sanitized, though keeping a dangerous edge, as played by 40 year old Warner Baxter.

In Old Arizona is listed as the very first western talkie, although Leo Maloney may say differently if he could. Never-the-less it did break epic ground by being the first sound western made by a major studio (Fox Film Corporation) to use actual locations in Arizona, California and Utah.

Director/actor Raoul Walsh was set to direct and star as the Cisco Kid. After shooting a few long shots of Walsh riding a horse as Cisco a freak accident happened costing him the role and his right eye. While driving back to Los Angeles from location in Utah a rabbit jumped into the windshield. Footage of Walsh riding in long shots remained in the film. Irving Cummings took over as director while Walsh recuperated. From then on Walsh would settle into a very successful directing career while wearing his trademark eye patch. As a side-note, safety glass was added to cars the year following the accident.

"B" western star Buddy Roosevelt was then signed for the role. It might have been his shot at the big time, but it wasn't to be. Shortly before he was to report for filming he broke his leg. Poor Buddy would go on to star in westerns with increasingly lower budgets. His bad luck continued when Monogram Pictures wanted to sign him for a series of low budget westerns. His wife demanded too much money from the studio and the deal fell through. After that Buddy would continue to act into the 1960s usually in uncredited roles.

Warner Baxter had been in films since 1914, the same year Cisco first came to the screen as played by William R. Dunn. By 1928 he had worked his way up the acting ladder to matinee idol. Starring roles would continue for Baxter through the 1930s although as time went on they tended to be "B" films. From 1943 through '49, Baxter would comfortably settle into the 2nd feature niche as "Crime Doctor" in a series of ten films for Columbia Pictures.

In Old Arizona was released in 1929 and was intended as a stand-alone film. However, the popularity of Baxter- not to mention being a feature length sound film—catapulted it into a winner and a prime candidate for further adventures.

Baxter would go on to win the Academy Award for his portrayal. Other nominations for the Oscar included Best Picture and Best Director for which Irving Cummings won for a picture that Raoul Walsh was set to direct before his accident.

The following year saw Baxter return to the same territory for Fox although not as the Cisco Kid. *The Arizona Kid* was definitely aiming for the same crowd without using the Cisco Kid label. This time Utah and California stood in for Arizona.
In 1931 Baxter again returned as a Cisco type character in the all-star short film *The Stolen Jools* released by Paramount. That same year he officially returned for Fox as the O. Henry character in *The Cisco Kid* – named as such so fans knew they were getting the real deal.

This film was shot just outside Tucson, Arizona as well as the Iverson Ranch in the L.A. area. Edmund Lowe returned as Sergeant Mickey Dunn, a "friendly" advisory to the kid. It would also be the first time that Chris-Pin Martin would show up as Cisco's early film sidekick, Gordito.

In 1936 Baxter would once again play a "Cisco Type" in *The Robin Hood of Eldorado*. This time out he played Joaquin Murrieta for Metro-*Goldwyn*-Mayer, probably hoping to seize on Fox and Baxter's success with the Cisco Kid films.

Although it was reminiscent of Cisco, it was supposedly based on Murrieta's biography and was filmed as a follow-up to Metro's successful bio-pic *Viva Villa* filmed two years before. Future Pancho, Leo Carrillo, co-starred in *Viva Villa*. 1936 would be the pinnacle of Baxter's career when he was listed as the highest paid actor in Hollywood.

Surprisingly, Fox wouldn't return to Cisco until 1939 when a fifty year old Baxter would play the role one more time in the aptly titled *The Return of the Cisco Kid*.

Chris-Pin Martin once again returned as Gordito while another up and coming actor, Cesar Romero, would also ride alongside Warner as "Lopez." During the interim Fox and 20th Century had joined together to form 20th Century Fox, making it one of the biggest Hollywood studios.

By 1939 series films were becoming very popular with the major studios. MGM had the Andy Hardy, Tarzan, Dr. Kildare and Thin Man series. 20th Century Fox already had successful series entries with Chinese detective Charlie Chan and Japanese Interpol detective, Mr. Moto, so why not a western hero?

The Mr. Moto series was discontinued in 1939 due to strained relationships with Japan and Charlie Chan would be sold to Monogram Pictures within 5 years. 1939 was prime for a new film series so why not a character the studio had been toying with for a decade?

Return of the Cisco Kid was filmed completely on the 20th Century Fox lot unlike the first two Baxter films, obviously a series budget move. With the success of the previous films it was a certain series bet, but would a much older Baxter be acceptable in the role? The answer came just eight months later with the release of *The Cisco Kid and the Lady*. Chris-Pin Martin would return as Gordito, but this time Cisco was played by dashing thirty-two year old Cesar Romero, one of the Cisco's sidekicks from the previous film.

Romero gave it a certain legitimate Latin flare. Born of Cuban parents in 1907 Manhattan, Cesar would have a long successful career in film and television. His main claim to fame today comes from playing 'The Joker' on the 1960s *Batman* TV series. So famous was this "Latin from Manhattan" and his mustache that he refused to shave it for his TV role. "Look closely and you'll see the mustache under his Joker make-up.

Romero, along with Chris-Pin Martin would appear in 6 series films between 1939 and 1941. In order they were: *The Cisco Kid and the lady* (1939), *Lucky Cisco Kid* (1940), *Viva Cisco Kid* (1940), *The Gay Caballero* (1940), *Romance of the Range* (1941) and *Ride on Vaquero* (1941).

Note the titles. It's interesting to see that by the fourth film in the Romero series they stopped using 'Cisco' in the credits. Studios would do this when they were thinking of making a change with a film series or discontinuing it altogether. Just look at the Charlie Chan and Mr. Wong series for Monogram, or Universal's Sherlock Holmes series with Basil Rathbone and you'll see what I mean. The change came in 1941 when 20th Century Fox discontinued the series. But it wasn't to be the end of Cisco—however it was the end for Gordito.

In 1945, after nearly a three year hiatus, the appropriately named *The Cisco Kid Returns*—not to be confused with the earlier ***Return of The Cisco Kid***—was released by Poverty Row studio Monogram Pictures. They purchased the rights after 20th Century Fox discontinued the series just as they had with Charlie Chan.

The Cisco Kid Returns would introduce the Pancho character played by Martin Garralaga as well as the first appearance of Duncan Renaldo as Cisco. Two more Cisco Kid films were released in 1945, ***The Cisco Kid in Old New Mexico*** (is that title an oxymoron?), and ***South of the Rio Grande***. The remaining Monogram films were void of using Cisco Kid in the title. The final five released by United Artists would never mentioned Cisco in any title. Duncan Renaldo made a career of playing Latinos, Russians, Italians, any type of ethnic character. This was due to the fact that studios in those days felt that an accent, no matter what the foreign dialect, would fool the theater audience. This could possibly be true in Renaldo's case. He's mostly known as a Latin even though his accent was that of Eastern Europe.

Renaldo's past was shrouded in a bit of mystery and studio bios didn't help untangle his origins. What we do know is that he was born Renault Renaldo Duncan in 1904 and that his origins were Romanian—although other sources say Spain or New Jersey.

Even his name has an air of mystery in that the surname 'Duncan' is of Gaelic origin and not Romanian or Latin. Renaldo would often tell people that he never knew his biological parents or where he was actually born. He did say that his earliest memories were of Romania. It's more than likely his birth place couldn't have been New Jersey due to his arrest in 1934 for being in the United States illegally. Renaldo would say that he was stranded in the states when a Brazilian ship he was working on caught fire. He was left on his own with a 90-day seaman's permit. This was in the early 1920s and he spent the next decade in the states eventually finding film work.

He would spend a year in prison before Herbert Yates, president of the newly formed Republic Pictures, came to his rescue. President Roosevelt stepped in as well and gave him a full presidential pardon. This would serve both Renaldo and Yates well when Republic Pictures signed the actor to a seven year contact in 1937.

By the time he was signed to play The Cisco Kid, Renaldo was no stranger to playing a Latin in a western series. He had already played Renaldo/Rico Rinaldo as part of the Three Mesquiteers series in 1939 and '40 under his Republic Pictures contract.

Along the way he also supported The Lone Ranger (Robert Livingston), Allan Lane, Hopalong Cassidy, and Gary Cooper to name a few.

Two more Cisco Kid films were released in 1945, the aforementioned *The Cisco Kid in Old New Mexico* and *South of the Rio Grande*. You might say that Renaldo's appearance in 1945 was the start towards the successful television series a few years later but you would be wrong. Renaldo, complete with moustache, would continue the role more or less the way Cesar Romero had as a lovable but sometimes unethical rogue.

These initial three films in the series were filmed and released in 1945. By 1946 fans saw a new Cisco Kid, Gilbert Roland. Born in Mexico in 1905, Roland returned the character to more of the Warner Baxter type. Whereas, Romero and Renaldo were more the unethical romantics, Roland played him more like Baxter with a bit more danger and a tempered amount of shadiness.

Roland smoked, he drank, and he womanized. Basically Gilbert Roland was playing Gilbert Roland as he did in most of his films. None of the next six even hinted of Cisco in the title.

In *The Gay Cavalier* (1946), Pancho was replaced by a new sidekick simply called "Baby" played by Nacho Galindo. Martin Garralaga would return in the Roland films but as different featured characters. After the first film in this series Galindo was replaced by Frank Yaconelli for the next three, *South of Monterey* (1946), *Beauty and the Bandit* (1946), and *Riding the California Trail* (1947). For Roland's last two, *Robin Hood of Monterey* and *Beauty and the Bandit* - both released in 1947 - 'Baby' was replaced by the second 'Pancho,' Chris-Pin Martin.

The history of the Cisco Kid on screen continued the next year with a new producer and a not so new Cisco. The very independent Inter-American Productions took the reins making a deal with United Artists to release their Cisco Kid films.

This would be the series that changed the look and style of the Kid edging him closer to television. Duncan Renaldo returned as Cisco and would now play a family friendly rogue sans moustache. It's also been said that the change was made at the insistence of Renaldo himself.

Inspiration took hold and Leo Carrillo was signed to play Pancho. Despite the broken accent Carrillo would use in many of his film roles, he was born in 1881 in Los Angeles, California to an affluent family—Leo's father had been the first mayor of Santa Monica.

He was a newspaper cartoonist before turning to acting on the New York Stage, definitely a place where an actor's diction must be understood, and then film starting in 1927. In all Carrillo appeared in over 90 films before his death in 1961. And yes– in case you're wondering - Leo Carrillo State Park/Beach is named after him due to his conservation efforts.

Although Carrillo was extremely well known by 1948 it was a bit of a risk to hire the 67 year old actor for a possibly strenuous role.

Again there is no mention of The Cisco Kid in the titles of these films. *The Valiant Hombre* was the only film in this new series to be released in 1948, but 1949 saw *The Gay Amigo*, *The Daring Caballero* and *Satan's Cradle* in quick succession. The final entry in the official Cisco Kid series, *The Girl from San Lorenzo* was released in 1950. With each entry in this final series of films Pancho and Cisco were developing into the characters we would know on the TV show. The final film was also the first time Renaldo would wear the famous Cisco Kid costume. As a matter of fact, the final film was released in February of 1950 and the TV series started on September 5th of the same year. It was a very smooth transition.

ZIV Television produced the series which aired in first run syndication from 1950 until 1956. Frederick Ziv was a successful advertising agency owner and radio syndicator when he recognized that the fresh television market would be looking for new productions to air outside the network primetime programs—there were also independent TV stations which would need programing. Setting up an independent syndication production company Ziv would market his programs to local sponsors and stations wanting to break into television. The ploy was a success. Each show was produced on a low budget of around $30,000, making it profitable for ZIV, the local stations airing the shows and the sponsors. Other ZIV productions included *Highway Patrol*, and *Sea Hunt*.

Because the last set of films with Renaldo and Carrillo set the template for television there wasn't much tampering with the characters except, like many of the early TV westerns, they aimed to appease the younger crowd while maintaining the older audience as well.

Surprisingly *The Cisco Kid* was the very first television series shot completely in color—originally 16mm and later in 35mm to appease network affiliates who began to air the show.

In 1950 color shows weren't broadcast nor were color TV sets available on the market and wouldn't be really necessary for avid viewers for more than another decade. This showed great foresight on Frederick Ziv's part for future syndication possibilities.

In other media such as radio The Cisco Kid and Pancho had been riding together since 1942. The radio show would continue into 1956 the same year the TV show ceased production. It was on the radio show that the famous final words on every show,

"Oh Pancho" "Oh Ceesco" were first spoken and made even more famous by the TV show.

Technically Duncan Renaldo and Leo Carrillo rode the range together through 156 episodes. However, in 1953 while shooting the fourth season episode, **Battle of Red Rock Pass**, Renaldo was seriously injured when a huge prop rock was pushed down a hill at Cisco.

Although made from lightweight material the rock gained momentum as it rolled down the hill and hit Renaldo directly on the head resulting in a broken neck. The star successfully mended from the serious injury but missed out in visibly appearing for nine episodes.

The writers went to work and created a scenario where a double was used for Renaldo as well as stock footage. The double was disguised wearing masks as a ghost, while Renaldo recorded his lines from his hospital bed wearing a weight suspended from the back of his head.

By the time the show ended, Renaldo was 52 and Carrillo was 75 but they never showed it on TV or their dozens of personal appearances. Pancho and Cisco were fully developed with the final series of films and made the smooth transition to the small screen.

Renaldo and Carrillo had great chemistry and that made their adventures so much fun to watch for both adults and new children fans.

In 1951, at the 3rd Annual Emmy Awards, the show was nominated for an Emmy for Best Children's Show against another western favorite *The Lone Ranger*—they lost to *Time for Beany*.

In 1994, a television film was made and aired on the TNT Network. Jimmy Smits played Cisco with Cheech Marin perfectly cast as Pancho. The film was one of the few times characters from 1950s television were updated while still keeping the flavor of the original right down to the "Oh Pancho," "Oh Ceesco."

Altogether Cisco and Pancho rode Diablo and Loco through 6 seasons and 156 episodes. Today, as of this writing, *The Cisco Kid* television series can be found on every type of visual medium there is. From the old television set, to the Internet, to all other forms of video we can still hear that familiar,

Cisco: *"Good Bye, Amigos!"*

Pancho: *"See you soon!"*

Indeed you will Cisco and Pancho, indeed you will.

***

CHAPTER SEVEN

Happy Trails... Finally!

Trailing the posse when it came to television was the King of the Cowboys and the Queen of the West. But Roy and Dale had a tremendous run for 6 seasons, December 30th, 1951 to June 9th 1957 with *The Roy Rogers Show* before it continued well into the 1960s on Saturday mornings.

Roy's success was bittersweet however when compared to Gene and Hoppy and the empires they built around their shows. Most of the trouble would be caused by Roy's one time savior, Herbert J. Yates.

If Harry "Pop" Sherman had been more like Yates then William Boyd might never been a success with a Hopalong Cassidy TV series. And Autry was totally free of the grasp of the

Republic Picture's president when he began his Flying "A" Production Company.

So resentful was Roy of Yates and his interference that over 40 years later while Roy was at home watching old film footage of a Republic Pictures picnic he spotted Yates playing with some studio employee's kids and made the comment, *"Well, what do you know, I have proof that the SOB was human."*

Like many Hollywood film producers, outwardly Yates saw television as an enemy to the film industry, but privately entered into an agreement to sell or lease old Republic films to the local markets at varying prices depending on market size.

The showing of these syndicated packages, much like the block buying practices of old, where a welcome deal for local stations who didn't have the money to hire labor and talent nor buy the expensive equipment for running local live television. It also added to the pockets of studios like Republic because the larger stations didn't have a coast to coast linkup via a coaxial cable for immediate coast to coast broadcasting.

To former studio stars like Sunset Carson or Don "Red" Barry this gave them a shot in the arm to briefly repackage themselves through other Gower Gulch studios to produce low budget westerns trying to regain some of the Republic gloss. To actors like Allan "Rocky" Lane still under contract to Republic it was a mixed blessing. To Roy Rogers, who wanted nothing more than to gravitate towards TV, it was a matter of terrible timing that could undermine his worth on the market and tip his hand before the time was right.

Yates had an ironclad rule that no Republic Pictures contract player would ever appear on television, except for the library of films he was offering.

The studio president made one exception and agreed to let Roy appear on his old sidekick, Gabby Hayes', show from New York City, on which Roy made a big deal of thanking Herbert J. Yates for letting him do it.

Recently I asked Roy and Dale's daughter, Cheryl Rogers-Barnett about the appearance and the acknowledgment. *"Yates must have made Dad say it. I can't think of any other reason why he would have done it."*

It also came around the time for Roy to renew his contract with the studio. But he had one stipulation. In order for him to stay on and do films Yates had to let Roy do his television show as well.

Battle lines were drawn. Yates knew if he lost the war he could possibly be blamed for a flood of contracted film stars breaking contracts and entering television before the studios could take advantage themselves.

He had already been down this road with Gene and had lost. He wouldn't let it happen with Roy. Just as he had done with Autry in his last series of Republic films, Yates saddled Roy with his worst sidekick ever, Pinky Lee.

Lee was a stage comic known for his off-color humor, so it was very odd that in 1954 he would have his own Emmy nominated children's programs. It's been said that his show was the inspiration for *Pee-Wee's Playhouse*.

Roy carried on through this last series of films while trying to fight the potential sell of the studio backlog of his films knowing it would hurt his chances to make a good deal for a new television program.

During the time that Roy was contending with Yates off screen and Pinky Lee on screen, Quaker Oats pulled their sponsorship from Roy's radio show fearing they might get caught in the crosshairs of any court litigation between Republic Pictures and Roy Rogers Enterprises. Roy needed some good news.

In the past, Yates had tried to stop Roy from walking out on a contract by telling him he couldn't take Trigger—Roy balked, he owned Trigger, or that unlike Gene Autry, Roy Rogers wasn't his real name, but Roy balked at this as well. Now it was Roy's turn to use the same ploy by claiming that his library of films couldn't be sold by Yates because Roy alone was the owner of his stage name and likeness. Gene had signed a contract with Republic in 1938 which gave him all rights to his likeness in merchandising, Roy reportedly followed suit years later.

Feeling confident that he would win in the matter, Roy filed a restraining order to prevent Yates from selling his films to television. The matter would now go to court. Roy then made an agreement with NBC to advance him $100,000.00 to produce four half hour episodes of *The Roy Rogers Show*.

Production started July 1st 1951. Roy and his legal team worked around the clock on the four episodes getting their ducks in a row for court while seeking a sponsor for the show. It was an exhaustive time but things seemed to be looking up when General Foods agreed to sponsor the TV show, but only if Roy won his case.

During this time he also signed his first major independent film contract to co-star with Bob Hope and Jane Russell in Paramount Pictures *Son of Paleface*, which was to start shooting on August 1st of 1951.

On October 18th, 1951 the victory was handed to Roy when an injunction was handed down forbidding Republic Pictures from selling any of his films to television. However, as with anything in life, nothing is forever. In June 1954 the ruling was overturned on appeal. A verdict now in favor of Republic Pictures found that they could indeed sell the films in question to television. However, by then *The Roy Rogers Show* had been a successful television show since its December 1951 debut.

The victory in '51 was not without its battle scars. So depleted was Roy Rogers Enterprises that there wasn't much left to produce the show on a week to week basis. *"Didn't you ever wonder why there were no songs on the show?"* Cheryl Rogers-Barnett asked me. *"It's because Mom and Dad spent so much money fighting Yates."*

It's true that outside of Roy and Dale ending each show with Dale's recently penned *Happy Trails to You* the episodes are pretty much void of singing. Cheryl would go on to say that production budgets were tight and left no room to pay for musical numbers. In all, songs can be heard in, *The Feud*, *Empty Saddles*, and *Ginger Horse*, three out of 100 episodes.

The show itself took a very simple approach. Whereas, Gene would appear in different locales from week to week giving the appearance of mini-features, Roy set his show squarely in fictitious Mineral City located in a wondrous place named Paradise Valley much like the make-believe west of Republic Pictures where different time periods would blend together to become its own reality.

Roy was, of course, ranch owner Roy Rogers. Dale Evens was—'wink wink'—platonic owner of the Eureka Café, and sidekick Pat Brady, was Dale's cook. While Roy would ride Trigger and Dale would ride Buttermilk, Pat drove Nellybelle—actually Roy's real jeep he would use at the Double R Bar Ranch. And let's not forget the 'Wonder Dog' Bullet, the German Shepherd. Throughout my childhood I would name all my dogs Bullet, even though they were dachshunds.

Samuel Goldwyn Studios was used for interior shots while Iverson Movie Ranch was used for most of the exterior shots. Keeping the locals at a minimum was great for keeping the budgets down.

After leaving NBC the show was made available by CBS for Saturday morning reruns in the 1960s. It had a cheery atmosphere as opposed to the dark genre attitude of Gene's show—even though his show too was geared towards the family. For the longest time, in my mind, I remembered growing up watching the reruns thinking the show was in color, which wasn't the case throughout its entire run. Funny the things you remember from your childhood.

Today, it's entertaining to go back and watch the fun in Mineral City as the cowboys, with their six guns, drive cars, use phones, and have electric lighting, much like Roy's Republic Pictures films. But as an adult I now appreciate the tone that Gene put in his program that made each show so different, much like his Columbia Pictures films.

A confusing aspect of the two shows is the sidekicks. Originally Pat Buttram had a different name in each episode like in the films. When this became too difficult for Gene to keep track of, he was simply given his own name to use.

Likewise, when Pat Brady on occasion was handed sidekick duties to Roy in his films he was known as 'Sparrow Biffle.' That too would change for *The Roy Rogers Show* where he was simply Pat Brady. Still today you'll hear people mix the two up.

In 1955, *The Roy Rogers Show* was nominated for an Emmy for Best Western or Adventure Series. It lost to *Stories of the Century* with Jim Davis, almost 25 years before he became famous as Jock Ewing on *Dallas*.

That same year, Roy would try his hand at producing another television show. *Brave Eagle* starring Keith Larson. The 26 episodes would run from September 28th, 1955 through March 14th, 1956 on CBS.

One interesting aspect about this program is that it ran on CBS, but Roy's production company Frontiers Incorporated produced it through NBC. The show probably didn't have a chance from the start as it aired opposite the second half of ABC's *Disneyland* which over the years went through many different title changes.

RIDING the HOLLYWOOD TRAIL II

On September 29, 1962, *The Roy Rogers and Dale Evans Show*—a western variety program premiered on ABC television and ran for thirteen weeks. By this time *The Roy Rogers Show* was now running on Saturday mornings on CBS and was a hit. The variety show aired against the extremely popular *Jackie Gleason Show* also on CBS in prime time. As his earlier show had premiered on December 30th, 1951, Roy and Dale's variety show left the air on December 29th, 1962.

Of the big three, Gene, Hoppy and Roy, the latter had the most to lose. Hoppy had already tested the waters with his edited films, Gene was still in the film business with Columbia Pictures when he made the move to television, but Roy had burned his bridges with Republic and fought for his rights against the motion picture industry by taking his former studio to court. True, Republic did win the right to show his films on TV a few years later, but Roy won the right to produce a very well received television show that ran for years and years and today is still enjoyed by millions of fans old and new.

It's nice to know—no matter what the price—that the good guy wins in the end.

***

CHAPTER EIGHT

Following the Television Hollywood Trail

Although Gene, Roy, Hopalong Cassidy, The Lone Ranger and The Cisco Kid were the most notable and successful western stars or characters to follow the Hollywood Trail into television, there were others who also rode into programs with varying degree's of success. Some were able to pull off the switch with interesting variations on their screen personalities, while others for one reason or another simply failed to make the cut and were out of town by sundown.

Tim McCoy had been one of the 'Big Five' western stars of the silent era – the others being Hoot Gibson, Ken Maynard, Buck Jones, and Tom Mix. Like the other four, Tim survived the change to talkies and would have a successful career in 'B' westerns well into the 1940s.

Meet the Colonel

In February of 1950, the unlikely though interesting Colonel Tim McCoy took the big step into live television with– what else—***The Tim McCoy Show***. He had made the move successfully from silent film to sound and now he was attempting the same with television. This half hour show aired locally in Los Angeles, California on early Saturday evenings with the basic premise that Tim would relate historical stories of the old west based on both fact and fiction.

Iron Eyes Cody (Espera Oscar de Corti) would join Tim on the show along with Native American entertainers and tribes to give the viewer's lessons about their culture. Tim was actually an expert in sign language and would give a lesson each week. The reason for Tim's passion was easy to understand if you knew his background. Without going into his extensive rodeo career, decorated military service, the fact that he had worked with Native Americans speaking several dialects and was an expert with sign language, Tim had a fascinating life by the time he hit the film industry.

He started his film career by coming in through the back door when Jesse Lasky, head of Famous Players – Lasky (within five years it would become Paramount Pictures) asked him to provide Native Americans for the 1923 film *The Covered Wagon*. Lasky also asked Tim to serve as the technical advisor.

Tim also provided the studio with Native Americans to come to Hollywood and entertain the audience in movie theaters before the film. Word got around and Tim was asked if he would take the group on a tour in Europe? It was a very successful trip and Tim's reputation was becoming something that the film studios began to take notice of.

After returning home from the tour, big time MGM producer Irving Thalberg asked him to sign a contract with the studio for a series of films.

Tim would also appear in films for Universal later on in the era and appear for the studio in their first sound serial *The Indians are Coming!* Tim had a nice pleasant voice with very proper elocution that somewhat betrayed his rough riding background. His acting was standard and he successfully made the change to sound.

By 1938, Tim could be found in Gower Gulch making low budget programmers for Columbia Pictures and other Poverty Row studios. After appearing with Buck Jones and Raymond Hatton in the Three Mesquiteers knock-off Rough Riders series for Monogram Tim retired from the screen in 1942.

He decided to run for the Republican nomination for senator of Wyoming. He lost the bid and then surprisingly volunteered for active duty in the U.S. Army. Being in his early fifties this didn't seem like the best move but he was passionate about serving and had maintained his active reserve commission since World War One, where he had served with the Army Air Corp and Army Air Forces. Because of this he was accepted. During World War Two, he served in Europe where he received numerous decorations.

Although he would make cameo appearances in films, *Around the World in 80 Days* in 1956, *Run of the Arrow* in 1957, and *Requiem for a Gunfighter* in 1965—which featured many 'Golden Age of Film Western Stars' like, Bob Steele, Johnny Mack Brown, Rod Cameron, Raymond Hatton, and Dick Jones—Tim pretty much retired from films after his service.

In 1950, Tim decided to try his hand at live TV. His 30 minute show featured Native Americans who would perform and speak of their heritage. After this 30 minute local television show finished each week, KTLA television—which aired the program—would show one of Tim's films from Gower Gulch Studios, Monogram, Victory, Puritan or Producers Releasing Corporation (PRC).

The early days of television had not only upstart independent local stations looking for shows to fill their schedule but the major networks affiliates as well. CBS, NBC, ABC and Dumont were searching for recognizable personalities and Tim McCoy fit the bill.

In 1952, the CBS affiliate KNXT began to air Tim's show and this is what many information sites list as his first television program. This 30 minute program ran through March of '53 without the following movie.

KNXT also gave Tim a weekday show called, **Tim McCoy's Wild West**, where he would simply talk about the real west and what it was like. Basically a lecture series. Tim's shows pretty much were geared toward kids since the beginning and in 1953 he won a local Emmy for 'Best Kids Show." It was quite an honor, but it was surrounded by a bit of controversy when Tim refused to attend the awards ceremony. The reason? His competition was a local kid's show featuring a duck, **Webster Webfoot**. Tim's own words about the subject, *"I'll be damned if I'm going to sit there and get beaten by a talking duck,"* kind of said it all.

From there Tim would experiment with other formats including a pilot for an action television show called **The Tim McCoy Show**. The name of the pilot episode was **Deadwood Days**. The 15 minute pilot was shot in color and also featured Iron Eyes Cody and Elisha Cook, Jr.

The announcer introduced Tim as, *"America's favorite story teller."* The premise was that Tim would wonder through a room, picking up old west props which would cause Tim to reminisce while clips from vintage westerns were shown. This show was picked up and ran for 39 episodes from 1953 through 1954.

But Tim wasn't done yet. He was 64 years old when he did a pilot for a full-fledged action TV western series called **Indian Agent**.

For this show Tim went back to a character he played in a series of films back in the 1930s. For seven films released from 1936 through 1939 Tim rode as 'Lightning' Bill Carson. Tim took pride in his ability to disguise Lightning Bill as Asian and Hispanic characters—much like The Lone Ranger would play old prospectors, etc. in order to catch the bad guys. Unfortunately he wasn't as good and is embarrassing to watch these days. Most of the films were released by Victory and produced by an uncredited Sam Katzman.

No matter what his age, it would have been good to see Colonel Tim McCoy back in the saddle, but it wasn't to be. The pilot didn't sell. Fortunately the pilot does exist. Unfortunately it's in a private collection and isn't available for viewing.

Today his TV shows wouldn't hold much interest except for Western fans. However for the early to mid-1950s, Colonel Tim McCoy rode the television Hollywood Trail.

Yer Darn Tootin'

Avid western fans know when they hear those words its George 'Gabby' Hayes. After Gabby left Republic Pictures he went on to support his best friend Randolph Scott in a couple of westerns before retiring from the big screen in 1950.

That same year *The Gabby Hayes Show* debuted on December 11th in New York City for NBC three times per week at 5:15pm. In those days New York was the huge hub of activity for television production with most of the quality live programing emanating from there.

The show was sponsored by Quaker Oats which would give Gabby a reason to warn viewers to "Watch out for yer televisionary sets," as he would fire a loaded cannon full of oats at the camera – or so we thought. The slogan for Quaker Oats was "shot from guns" – no one ever stopped to ask why a Quaker was shooting anything from a cannon to begin with?

There was no mistake that the show was aimed squarely at children. Gabby used his screen persona – a gift for gab and tall stories – keeping the young viewers entertained while whittling a piece of wood. Then he would show an extremely edited programmer western usually from the PRC corral and featuring Al 'Fuzzy' St. John as the comical sidekick to Buster Crabbe or Lash LaRue. It's interesting to note that one of the most famous sidekicks was introducing edited films starring what many would say was a chief competitor. I cover more on the sidekicks in the first *Riding the Hollywood Trail*.

It preceded *The Howdy Doody Show* which was an evening show at that time. It's also interesting to note that the floor manager for *The Howdy Doody Show* was a young Fred Rogers. Many of you will remember him from *Mr. Rogers Neighborhood*. So highly thought of was *The Gabby Hayes Show* that it was nominated for an Emmy for Children's Programming in 1953. The winner was the very popular live show *Time for Beany*, later turned into the cartoon show, *Beany and Cecil*.

This particular version of *The Gabby Hayes Show* left the air on January of 1954. During this period Gabby was also pulling double duty on *Howdy Doody*. Buffalo Bob Smith had a massive heart attack and was recuperating while Gabby briefly filled in.

But that wasn't the end of Gabby's television adventures. He returned to TV for a half hour version of his show which ran Saturday mornings on ABC. The program lasted 3 months, May, June, and July. After that, George 'Gabby' Hayes bid farewell to show business after 54 years of doing what he loved.

Gabby's name did live on for a while in comic book form and a New York Children's Summer Camp was named after him.

As for George Hayes private citizen, after his wife passed away in 1957, he lived in an apartment building that he owned and managed in North Hollywood until his death at the age of 83. There was the Big Three of Sidekicks, Smiley Burnette, Al 'Fuzzy' St. John and George 'Gabby' Hayes. Of them all, Gabby to this day is the most recognizable and that's because his appeal was and is so universal.

Lash Of the West

Lash LaRue was definitely a matter of taste – you either liked him or you didn't. Some could take him in small doses, but to have him up close in your living or family room every week might have been a bit much. He wasn't exactly a personable character like Roy, Gene or Hoppy.

Never-the-less, ABC ran the 15 minute syndicated *Lash of the West* on Sundays from January 1953 through April, 1953.

The gimmick with **Lash of the West** was that he was a modern day marshal named…wait for it…Lash LaRue
showing heavily edited PRC westerns featuring Lash and Fuzzy.

Each week modern day Marshal Lash LaRue would begin to tell a tale of his old west lawman grandfather named Lash LaRue as heavily edited versions of Lash's old films began to unfold on the tube. It had to fit a 15 minute format, complete with wraparound of present day Lash and an occasional guest. This meant that even an hour programmer western would lose much of its continuity.

This also means that for a brief time Lash would have been on ABC with his films while NBC's **The Gabby Hayes Show** was showing heavily edited versions of his films. He may have been, up to that point, the first actor to be appearing on two different channels in the same week with the same format.

As stated above, it didn't last long. First run it was on Sunday night at 6:30 EST from January 4th to April 26th 1953, although reruns would show up through the next January. But that wasn't the end of Lash on TV. Lash would pop up usually playing a bad guy on shows like **26 Men** and **Judge Roy Bean** for Russell Hayden's production company.

A brief return to regular TV occurred when, as simply Al LaRue, he played Sheriff Johnny Behan in 1959 on **The Life and Legend of Wyatt Earp** when the show moved to Tombstone, Arizona.

He lasted in the role for five episodes before he was replaced by Steve Brodie. The story has always circulated that he and **Wyatt Earp** star Hugh O' Brian didn't get along.

I had some personal time with Hugh after a luncheon at Roy Rogers 100th Birthday Celebration in Victorville, California, so I asked him about Lash. Hugh said that he was aware of the stories, but they had been extremely overblown and he really had no problem with Lash. You could tell there was something there but he wasn't going to tell me. After that we said no more about it as I could see Hugh was being a gentleman about it.

Lash LaRue is one of those characters that had a very interesting life. He had three wives listed Barbara Fuller, Reno Browne, and Marion Carney, however his late son, Ron LaRue once told me that he possibly had as many as 13 or more marriages.

That alone would have kept Al "Lash" LaRue busy with his whip on the Hollywood Trail.

Getting Lucky

Russell Hayden (Hayden Michael Pate Lucid) never quite got the recognition he should have as a screen cowboy. For my money I wish he had been one of the Republic even Monogram or PRC stars on his own. For a while he had his own series for Columbia, but one of the aforementioned studios would have appreciated his value.

But the dye was cast when old Russ was selected to play the second and longest sidekick, "Lucky Jenkins," for Hopalong Cassidy - so strong a sidekick was Hayden that it was hard to replace him, even when Rand Brooks took on the role of

"Lucky" in the later films. He just seemed to work better when riding alongside someone else after working with "Hoppy."

There were attempts along the way to make Russell a first tier western star when Harry Sherman starred him in the Zane Grey film, **Knights of the Range** (1940). But then it was back to "Hoppy."

Once he left Hopalong Cassidy he moved over to Columbia aiding Charles Starrett pre-Durango Kid. He still was called "Lucky" but his last name would change from film to film in the eight picture series. Columbia did give him his own eight film series, again as "Lucky" except one film, with Dub "Cannonball" Taylor. Russell looked great in the saddle and proved that he could carry the action.

Surprisingly he next moved to Universal and played second fiddle to Tex Ritter. A starring feature, **Frontier Law** (1942) had him stepping into Tex's boots while Ritter recuperated from an injury. Fuzzy Knight and Dennis Moore shared Russell's usual second fiddle role.

For budget reasons Universal excised some of their cowboy stars in 1943. When it was all said and done the remaining cowboys were Rod Cameron and Kirby Grant.

One thing Russell had going for him was that the films he made for Columbia were spread out by the studio to be released from the fall of 1942 through the summer of 1944.

This means that Russell was appearing on screen in both the Columbia and Universal films pretty much at the same time. Something that benefited him during 1943 and '44 while he served in the Navy. These two years, while he was away serving his country, would be the only time in his career that he would appear in the Motion Picture Herald Poll of Top Ten Cowboy Stars at the Box Office.

However it didn't help him any with the studios when he returned home in 1945. Russell's momentum with the studios was gone. He was no Gene Autry who could serve his country and then resume his career.

Roy Rogers, and film bad guy Dick Curtis were among investors for a new movie location to be called Pioneertown, an innovative type of location where the buildings actually were interiors they could use—including a bowling alley and restaurant—still in use as of this writing.

It's an interesting location, east of the San Bernadino Mountains a few miles outside of 29 Palms, to visit and walk – we drove – the streets where people actually live in the homes that were built for filming. He eventually purchased more land south of Pioneertown where he would build "Hayden Ranch," for his productions.

1950 would be a busy year for Russ Hayden – I think we know him well enough by now to call him Russ. He would appear in one episode as "Marshal #1" of a live western action show called, ***The Marshal of Gunsight Pass***, along with Eddie Dean and Riley Hill appearing as marshals in separate episodes.

It was an unusual show aired from Iverson's Ranch that didn't last long and has very little written about it. We know there were 22 episodes that aired in primetime on ABC, live from Los Angeles, then transferred via Kinescope to other areas. Trying to do a live action western couldn't have been easy.

Critics felt it was archaic even by 1950 standards, but it must have seemed like a good idea at the time. It ran for 6 months so episodes must have been rerun, even though they were originally live.

Hayden had better luck when he teamed with former child actor Jackie Coogan in 1952 for *Cowboy G-Men*. The show was filmed at the Iverson Ranch and rumor has it that it was shot in some form of 3-D hoping TV would catch up with the process. It did, but not in time to help this show. The show was also shot in color.

Unfortunately, today only one episode of the program, *Salted Mines* is available in color. Obviously, for the time, a lot of money was put into this show.

Today saying that a show lasted only one season means 13 episodes if they're "lucky"—the pun is there if you look for it. However, in 1952 one season meant up to 39 episodes, which is indeed how many of these shows were filmed. Today *Cowboy G-Men* could be run each week for the better part of a year without repeats. You might think that just because the show survived only one season 1952/53 it wasn't popular. On the contrary, *Cowboy G-Men* garnered fifty percent of the viewing audience at the time.

Russ and a very miscast Coogan play Pat Gallagher and Stoney Crockett respectively. The show had a veritable who's who of western character actors and bad guys on the show like, Roy Barcroft, Tom Tyler, Lane Bradford, Myron Healy, Pierce Lydon, Rick Vallin, X Brands, Robert Lowery, Lyle Talbot – the kind of faces we miss so much today.

There were several producers on the show, but Russ Hayden produced 14 of the episodes, getting his feet wet for the next step in his career.

We also need to take a brief trail detour and mention an odd film series that he did in 1950 which consisted of 6 westerns in which he co-starred with Jimmy Ellison, and featured Fuzzy Knight and Raymond Hatton.

Ron Ormond, who saved Lash LaRue when he was finished at PRC, had a "great" idea to put the two most memorable Hopalong Cassidy sidekicks together in one series of films. They both used their nicknames from the Hoppy series along with their real last names to become "Lucky" Hayden and "Shamrock" Ellison. Actually it does sound like a great idea and is pulled off just fine, however production values hit an all-time low.

The 6 films were all shot in one month using the same actors for each film, many scenes for different films in the series were shot back to back. The patchwork films were directed by veteran Republic Pictures director Thomas Carr while Lippert Pictures released the finished product. Once all the footage was completed Carr would edit it all down into the 6 Westerns.

Three other main actors were featured in all the films—Raymond Hatton, Fuzzy Knight, and an up and coming young actress Betty Adams—who would soon be signed by Universal—International Pictures and change her name to Julia/Julie Adams. Knight and Hatton would play different characters both humorous and villainous in the films.

As Julie Adams would later tell me, "It was at the very beginning of my career and those films were made so quickly, I don't remember much about them, but they were a good training ground."

While still appearing from time to time in other actor's film and television endeavors, from here on Russ set his sights on producing.

Judge Roy Bean was filmed at Pioneertown and Hayden's own movie ranch in color. Syndicated shows were extremely popular in the 1950s and early '60s with independent stations and networks needing product to show outside of prime time. *Judge Roy Bean* was one prime example—although it was aimed squarely at a younger audience and whitewashed the judge greatly.

Hayden produced 17 of the 39 episodes and wrote two. The series was shot in 1956 and ran for the 1956/'57 season. Edgar Buchanan played the judge—a role that fit him much better than Red Connors in the Hoppy series. He was aided by Jack Beutel fitting nicely into the role of the young sidekick—a role the Hopalong Cassidy TV show could have used.

Beutel had an interesting but sad career in Hollywood. Signed by Howard Hughes, Beutel played Bill the Kid in the infamous *The Outlaw* which was filmed in 1941, but held up for release until 1943, partly due to censorship issues with Jane Russell's cleavage—something Hughes loved for the free advertising.

During this time and after the film's release Hughes refused to loan out the young actor. As a result Jack lost all momentum to his career and wasn't seen on screen again until 1951 as Bob Younger in ***Best of the Badmen*** with Robert Ryan.

He had only 4 more roles until he was cast in 1956 for ***Judge Roy Bean***, as Deputy Jeff Taggert/Taggart as the spelling changed from show to show—much as Jack's own real last name. Born Jack Allender Beutel his name would show up on film and TV credits as Buetel much of the time. After ***Judge Roy Bean*** there were only nine more credits before he retired in 1961.

If anyone had a good reason to detest Howard Hughes it's Jack Beutel. If he had more of a say about his career maybe he could have gone further—then again who knows, he was never given the chance.

26 Men is fondly remembered as a good example of a syndicated adult western. The show lasted for two seasons 1957-'59 with 78 episodes of which Russell Hayden was executive producer as well as being the co-writer of the memorable theme song for the show.

Tristram Coffin played the actual leader of the Arizona Rangers Captain Thomas H. Rynning while Clint Eastwood like Kelo Henderson placed Ranger "Clint"—yep—Travis. Guests ranged from Lash LaRue, Robert Blake, Edgar Buchanan, Gregg Palmer, and Doug McClure, to Dub Taylor, Glenn Strange, Denver Pyle, Leonard Nimoy and Deforest Kelly, before they even thought of ***Star Trek***.

So popular was this show that avid fans can still begin the theme song, if not finish it. Here goes, everybody sing:

CHARLIE LeSUEUR

Saddle up, Saddle up, Saddle up
This is the story of 26 Men
Who rode the Arizona Territory
High is the Glory of 26 Men
Whose parish helped to fill the territory
26 Men who saddled up and then
Rode out to answer duties call
26 Men who lived to ride again
And fight for the rights and liberty for all
This is the story of 26 Men
Enforcing law within the territory raise be the glory of 26 Men
Who rode the Arizona Territory. Ride on, Ride On, Ride On

Although we've spent far too long out of the book's time frame, mainly 1948 through 1956, and the end of the first western TV shows, **26 Men** was an important part of Russell Hayden's emergence as a producer. Russ would appear in only one episode of **26 Men** in 1957. He would produce a very low budget film **When Girls Take Over** with Robert Lowery, Marvin Miller, and former co-stars James Ellison and Jackie Cooper in 1960—released in 1962—that was filmed in Puerto Rico.

He wouldn't appear before the camera again until 1963 with **30 Minutes at Gunsite**, along with Marty Robbins and the Sons of the Pioneers, Lloyd Perryman, Dale Warren, Roy Lanham, Rusty Richards and in his last film performance, Pat Brady.

It was a pilot for a TV show shot in color, but it was never picked-up for production. Russell produced the show and appeared in a small role billed as the "Drifter."

Russell Hayden died at the age of 68 on June 9th, 1981, without really getting his just due as a western pioneer. I hope this chapter helps set things right just a bit.

Out of the Blue of the Western Sky . . .

Although Kirby Grant isn't really considered one of the cowboy stars of film - from what I've heard never wanted to be—he was one of Universal's cowpokes along with Rod Cameron.

He also played a western hero of sorts on early television—we knew him as Sky King. For 72 episodes and four seasons he soared through the western skies with his niece Penny and sometimes his nephew Clipper. Even though only 72 episodes were shot and only four seasons the show is credited for running from 1952 through 1961. Before we get to that, let's take a look at Kirby's history in film.

Kirby had received a scholarship to the American Conservatory of Music in Chicago as a violinist and singer. He would use his talent as a violinist from time to time on screen but it was his singing voice that got the attention of the studios.

Although he would dabble in westerns he was usually seen as a juvenile lead in support of the Mexican Spitfire, Dr. Kildare, Blondie, Abbott and Costello, and Olsen and Johnson - even appearing with Johnny Mack Brown at Monogram. Finally

100

he was picked as Universal's cowpoke for six films with Fuzzy Knight. The series ended in 1946 and he was back to playing bland romantic leads sometimes in a singing role.

1949 found Kirby at Monogram Pictures for a series of Mountie Films, usually as Corporal Rod Webb.

Television came calling in 1952 with a filmed version of a popular radio show and the character he would forever be associated with—*Sky King*. The radio show ran from 1946 through 1954 with various actors voicing the role, but never Kirby.

The premise for *Sky King* is simple. Schuyler "Sky" King lives on the Flying Crown Ranch with his niece Penny and sometimes his nephew, Clipper. The ranch is located in the fictional town of Grover, Arizona. During each episode Sky would use his plane, the Songbird, to help those in trouble. The Songbird had an extreme make-over during the run of the show for the first 39 episodes it was a Cessna T-50 while the rest of the episodes it appears to be a Cessna 310B.

As a side-note of how our past is disappearing. About 30 years ago I was taking the Universal tram tour. The guide turned our attention to an old battered barely recognizable airplane shell in some brush on the side of a hill. He told us that it was all that was left of Sky King's plane. It should have been in a museum somewhere or at the very least in storage—a sad ending for the Songbird.

The run of the television show is very interesting and can get confusing, so follow closely. *Sky King* began September 16th, 1951 on Sunday afternoon for NBC until October 26th,

1952. These episodes were rebroadcast Saturday mornings on ABC, November 8th, 1952 through September 21st, 1953. After that it made its Prime Time debut on Monday night for ABC. By August and September of 1954 it was being telecast twice a week with re- runs before it was canceled.

Sky King still had life and went into syndication in 1955 with new episodes. It ran in syndication with new episodes until March 8th, 1959. It had been a staple on both NBC and ABC before it went into syndication so it made sense that CBS would take a stab at it. They would show reruns of the show in the early afternoon on Saturdays for those on the east coast, but for us western kids it aired as part of the Saturday morning lineup. This continued until September 3rd, 1966— only 72 episodes and almost 16 years, a good healthy run in one form or another.

Kirby Grant would learn to embrace his legacy and often made himself available to fans, eventually thinking about reviving the show and have the ranch become a home for abandoned or orphaned kids, much like the real Sky King Youth Ranches he and his wife had founded.

One honor that Kirby Grant received was an invitation by the astronauts of the Space Shuttle Challenger to watch the launch to let him know how much *Sky King* had been a big influential part of their lives.

On his way to watch the launch, on October 30th, 1985, Kirby Grant was killed in an automobile accident—he was 73 years old—a strange occurrence for one who loved to soar in the blue of the western sky.

Roll Thunder Roll!

Red Ryder's failure to become a television show mystifies me. I hadn't planned on spending so much time on the two filmed pilots, but the misinformation surrounding them is surprising considering they're both available for viewing.

The two pilots, one with the last theatrical film actor to play the part Jim Bannon in 1951, and the second in 1955 with Allan "Rocky" Lane, who hadn't played the role since 1947, were well made but failed to sell. Unlike today, a show needed a large advertising sponsor to help fund their program. In the case of programs like the ones we've talked about it was companies like Kelloggs, Quaker Oats, Hostess, kid friendly commercial sponsors, whereas more adult programs would use cigarette, adult beverage, and other products geared for an older crowd.

Of all the cowboy characters from film, radio, and print, Red Ryder should have been an obvious choice to successfully make the leap to television, it just seemed like a winner.

Skipping over much of Red Ryder's history starting with Fred Harmon's popular comic strip which started in 1938 and getting right to the point, Red Ryder had been a very popular western film series for Republic Pictures, with both "Wild" Bill Elliott and Allan Lane.

Don Barry played the title character in the 12 chapter 1940 serial *The Adventures of Red Ryder*, directed by William Witney and John English. Barry wasn't an obvious choice to play a character that was tall and lanky, he personally felt he was wrong for the part and argued the point to no avail.

Standing at around 5'5", he had a beautiful head of hair but producers had Don wear a hair piece, reportedly to make his hair appear more red to match the comic strip although the serial was shot in black and white. He was also given a close resemblance to the character's costume complete with an oversized hat matching Red's in the strip but looking very strange on the diminutive Barry.

Witney would refer to him as "the Midget," and English didn't like working with Barry, only doing so in two more Republic westerns, *Dead Man's Gulch* and *Black Hills Express*, both in 1943.

Barry was scrappy by nature and reminded Republic Pictures of James Cagney, an actor he would continue to be compared to. Both the studio and Barry tried to use this to their benefit but it eventually became a burden for the actor.

The serial was a hit and Don Barry would forever be stuck with the nickname "Red," something he hated, but Republic Pictures continued to capitalize on the nickname in his series of westerns for them. Whenever possible he would insist on being billed as Donald Barry for other productions.

Barry was married to Republic contract player Peggy Stewart for a time. During the 1940s and '50s, Peggy played opposite every "B" western star of the time except her husband.

The Adventures of Red Ryder was a hit, primarily because Don Barry was so magnetic in it, but Republic didn't get around to making it into a western series until 1944.

Barry had been riding high as one of their top stars but he was also anxious to move on to more serious roles and wanted nothing more to do with Red Ryder, the studio was happy to concur. By 1944, Barry was no longer appearing in his own western series for the studio.

When it came time to make Red Ryder into a western series Don didn't want any part of it. He already had the nickname that he hated and wanted nothing more to do with the character.

Fortunately Republic had a star on the lot that was an even bigger name, more popular, and somewhat resembled the character—at least more than Barry. He was the 'peaceable man' William "Wild Bill" Elliott.

Elliott had already made his mark in "B" westerns at Columbia Pictures by the time he was signed at Republic and was one of the top stars for the studio who along with John Wayne were the only contracted western stars making "A" pictures for the studio. Elliott would bounce between "A" films as William Elliott and "B" films as "Wild Bill" Elliott.

Due to John Wayne's unexpected explosion as an "A" star after *Stagecoach* it became a necessity for Herbert Yates to rethink the whole budget system for his films.

In the past Republic would occasionally bring in "A" stars such as Richard Dix for *Man of Conquest* (1939), but now he needed to keep Wayne happy and so a new system was devised. *Dark Command* would be a step in that direction pairing the Duke with his *Stagecoach* co-star Claire Trevor and top actor Walter Pidgeon from MGM and directed by Raoul Walsh.

Republic now had four categories—"Jubilee," films shot for $50,000.00 in 7 days. "Anniversary," films shot in 14 to 15 days for $175,000 to $200.000. "Deluxe," major productions shot for $500,000.00 by in studio directors. And "Premiere," films shot by major directors like Walsh, Fritz Lang and John Ford which had a budget of $1,000,000.00 or more.

For example, Sunset Carson or Allan Lane would get "Jubilee," budgets, while Roy Rogers, and "Wild Bill" would have the "Anniversary," leaving the "A" budgets for William Elliott and John Wayne who would get "Deluxe" treatment except for those the Duke did with top directors like Ford, in that case they became "Premiere" productions. Gene Autry was not at Republic during much of this time.

Elliott proved quite popular as Red Ryder keeping his "Wild Bill" persona—complete with the "peaceable man" and gun handles forward in holster and a more reasonably sized hat.

Young Bobby Blake replaced Tommy Cook as Little Beaver and they were off and riding through sixteen films in the series starting in 1944. Gabby Hayes was in the first two films to assure the series would have a popular sidekick name to begin the series.

Allan Lane took over the role in 1946 along with Blake as Little Beaver. After seven more films in the series it came to an abrupt halt after a total of twenty-three films in four years.

The series was still popular, but a licensing dispute with the owners of the character ceased production. Republic Pictures had every intention of continuing the series, but the renewal date had been overlooked by the studio and the option wasn't picked up in time.

When the mistake was found, an increase in the asking price was demanded and the studio refused to pay the new asking price. Without missing a beat Republic stopped production on the series in 1947 and continued with Allan Lane becoming Allan "Rocky" Lane and Red Ryder's horse "Thunder" renamed "Black Jack." This series would continue through thirty-eight more films.

In 1949 independent film company Eagle-Lion bought the rights to the film series and made four more starring Jim Bannon.

The choice was actually inspired. Bannon looked close to the comic strip character, with a voice and demeanor very much like Bill Elliott's. Don Kay Reynolds, billed as "Little Brown Jug," was Little Beaver.

The Eagle-Lion Productions, although made on a shoe-string budget, were all shot in Cinecolor, an inexpensive two strip color process, with Bannon complete with red hair. After the four films were shot, Bannon would then go on to play sidekick to Whip Wilson in five films at Monogram.

These four Bannon films brought a close to Red Ryder on the big screen, but with the success of The Lone Ranger on television it seemed like Red Ryder would be a familiar favorite ripe for a weekly half hour show.

Jim Bannon would make a pilot in 1951 for a proposed Red Ryder TV series with an episode called *Whiplash*. Production values were not bad for the time and Bannon adopted a Red

Ryder type hat for the role with a single holster as opposed to the two he wore in his series. Casting Olive Carey, widow of legendary actor Harry Carey, Sr. to play Red Ryder's aunt, "The Duchess," was inspired for the low budget pilot.

One of the areas the pilot suffers is the absence of Don Kay Reynolds as Little Beaver. Bannon stated in his memoirs that the producers wouldn't meet Don's asking price to return to the role. Elsewhere it's been said that his schedule was too busy with rodeo appearances to do the pilot.

"Let just say it was a little bit of both," Don would tell me in a phone conversation. *"They hired a kid in Colorado to play the role and then had to re-dub his lines,"* Don would say. The role is billed in the credits as "Little Beaver played by Himself," and it's not really mentioned in any history of the Bannon pilot who the child actually was, except in error when he's referred to as being child actor Louis Lettieri.

Don, however, confirmed the real name and background of this little known Little Beaver. *"His real name is Kenny Pierce and he lives in New York State. He and his wife, Nancy, had a knife throwing act in Las Vegas for many years. Professionally he goes by Chi Chi Whitecloud."* So there you have it, finally the name of the fourth Little Beaver. Unfortunately there is no chemistry between Bannon and Pierce/Whitecloud. It's hard to imagine that if the pilot where indeed sold they would continue with this combination.

You'll find confusion on many information sites about this show actually going on for a full season. At the end of the pilot episode Jim Bannon speaks directly to the camera addressing any sponsors who might be interested in being the show's sponsor. He introduces the continuing characters on the show and refers to the 1st season episodes as if they had already been shot and edited. This may have caused confusion about it going for a whole season.

Another point of confusion may have been added to the mix by Pierce/Whitecloud as Don Kay Reynolds told me, *"I had this guy come up to me at a convention and say he was the last person to play Little Beaver and that he did a full season of episodes."*

If it was for the Bannon pilot then there are a few things wrong with what Pierce told Don. For instance, there were no more episodes filmed and just one more pilot in 1956 in which Louis Lettieri did indeed play Little Beaver.

One other miscalculation was the use of the radio's VO *"Roll Thunder!"* done with the same over done echo and reverb in the announcer's voice, possibly to remind people of The Lone Ranger's *"Hi Yo, Silver, Away!"* In the Bannon/Eagle-Lion films the phrase was used with a more natural voice and sounded perfectly fine. This mistake would be repeated with Lane's 1956 version as well. On radio it sounds fine, but on video it sounds forced and phony.

Bannon would continue to find steady work on TV. In 1955 he was Sandy North for twenty-six episodes of **The Adventures of Champion** for Gene Autry's Flying "A" productions, the company that would produce Allan "Rocky" Lane's Red Ryder pilot that same year. In 1957 he would appear on a regular basis as Sheriff Tynes on the **Casey Jones** series starring Alan Hale,

Jr. and Dub Taylor. He also appeared on episodes of *The Life and Times of Wyatt Earp*, *Mackenzie's Raiders*, *Jefferson Drum*, and *Buckskin* to name some of his western TV show appearances.

He was also the first husband of popular actress Bea Benaderet – *The Burns and Allan Show*, *The Flintstones* (Betty Rubble) and *Petticoat Junction*.

Bannon's *Red Ryder* pilot was just as good if not better than any western series in 1951, so it's a shame it wasn't given a chance.

In 1955, as westerns like *The Lone Ranger*, *Hopalong Cassidy*, and *The Cisco Kid* were winding down, another *Red Ryder* pilot was filmed featuring the last actor to play him at Republic Pictures, Allan Lane. Lane's last film as the character was in 1947, but he rode the celluloid range as Allan "Rocky" Lane at Republic until 1953.

Lane had lost none of his charm by 1955 when the pilot, *Gun Trouble Valley* was made. He also made no bother to look like Red Ryder.

If Little Beaver and the Duchess hadn't been in the pilot you might have thought he was simply playing "Rocky" Lane, as he was billed in the credits. If he had done the pilot a mere 5 years before it would have stood a good chance of selling.

Again the short coming is the need to constantly have the trademarked voice over from the radio show, "Roll Thunder," blare out every time Red rides off after the bad guys. It just doesn't fit the television medium, especially as more adult westerns were going into production.

The show is in black and white, as was Bannon's, but there's plenty of banter about the color of Red's hair color to let everyone know just where he got his nickname although Lane's familiar hairpiece was used.

Again, there was no sell, even though this pilot was produced through Gene Autry's Flying "A" Productions. With this production the answer as to why it didn't sell may have been simple. The time for this type of western had come and gone.

Both pilots are available for viewing. They're a must for vintage western fans.

It should be mentioned that the first series Red Ryder. "Wild Bill" Elliott also had two western pilots in the early 1950s, *The Marshal of Trail City* with Dub Taylor as Cannonball and *Parson of the West*.

Elliott had been working for Allied Artists—formerly Monogram—and shifted gears during the last three years of his film career, 1955 through '57 where he played modern day Detective Andy Doyle—Flynn in the 1st film.

Ironically, the very character that brought Bill Elliott to the attention of western fans, Wild Bill Hickok, started successfully riding the small screen range for eight season in 1951 in *The Adventures of Wild Bill Hickok*. What might have seemed like a natural for Elliott was instead played by a much younger Guy Madison with the popular Andy Devine as his sidekick Jingles P. Jones. Devine was everything a TV sidekick should be with his familiar gravely "Hey Wild Bill, Wait for me!" The show not only had a successful run on TV but on Mutual radio from 1951 to 1956.

As with many early television westerns *The Adventures of Wild Bill Hickok* went through a few production shifts along the line. Starting out as a syndicated show from 1951 through 1954. Starting in 1955, CBS continued the show through 1958, while ABC played reruns in 1957 and '58. The show was nominated for an Emmy as Best Western or Adventure Series in 1955 but lost out to *Stories of the Century* with a young Jim Davis.

Keeping in line with tradition Madison wore his six guns with butts out much like the real Wild Bill Hickok and "Wild Bill" Elliott did.

As far as Red Ryder, will he ever ride again on the big screen? Who knows, but his name has become famous due to the play and film, *When You Comin' Back Red Ryder?* and even more so in *A Christmas Story* where nine year old Ralphie Parker continually asks for a Red Ryder Carbine Action 200 shot Range Model air rifle.

***

EPILOGUE

The genesis of the pioneers of early television westerns is very much like that of the silent stars that either reinvented themselves for sound or failed.

In the case of Gene and Roy, they were the established royalty of "B" westerns, but they both had different approaches. While Gene wanted to remain more in line with his more down to earth Columbia films, Roy and Dale continued to produce light- hearted fare much like they did at Republic Pictures.

Gene had Pat Buttram and Champion to ride with him throughout the territory looking for adventure, while Roy and Dale stayed in Mineral City surrounding themselves with Pat Brady, Trigger, Buttermilk, and Bullet, the Wonder Dog—all the ingredients to make the young ones happy, and it worked for both of them.

William Boyd experimented with the formula until he came up with the half hour TV show. The idea that he should have continued with California and possibly Lucky is something to ponder. He realized that the show was lacking pizzazz at some point and asked Andy Clyde back, but he refused and so Boyd continued with Edgar Buchanan and the show looks very dated today.

The Cisco Kid had gone through so many changes over the years, but the last series of film adventures with Renaldo and Carrillo set the tone and the television show followed without missing a beat.

The Lone Ranger was a hard one. The serials were a definite "no" but they had the radio show to go by and Trendle had learned from dealing with Republic Pictures. He would be in control this time around. They fortunately found the right mix with Clayton Moore and Jay Silverheels, then lost it, and then found it again before it was too late.

We haven't even touched on Monte Hale or Rex Allen whom both tried their hand at different times. Monte never seemed to gain any momentum in film to carry him over to TV and was thus placed in the featured player category on TV. Rex didn't try his hand until 1958 and then with a series that was so different from his on screen persona that it lasted a little less than a year—***Frontier Doctor***—September 26, 1958, 20th, 1959.

Russell Hayden showed what a great talent he had onscreen and off, while Lash LaRue's faults may have done him in with bad temperament behind the scenes and a flat TV screen personality where, much different from motion pictures, the camera it right upon you in full close-up.

Unlikely survivors like Colonel Tim McCoy, and George "Gabby" Hayes provided terrific entertainment for the whole family for several years, proving there was still life after 60.

CHARILE LeSUEUR

Riding the Hollywood Trail: Tales of the Silver Screen Cowboys, told the story of those original film pioneers that made the move from silent films to the "talkies." Some survived, some didn't while studios fought the change not knowing what to do with this beast called sound. The cowboy stars showed the way—Buck, Tom, Hoot, Ken, Colonel Tim, and later John Wayne, Bob Steele, Tom Tyler, and Gene Autry.

The same story is true of the coming of television. Studios fought, but Hoppy, Gene, Cisco, Roy, The Lone Ranger, and even Colonel Tim, who had been there before, showed the way. The story is the same—but different.

* * * *

TIMBER CREEK PRESS

PHOTOS

Hopalong Cassidy from Film to Television

James Gleason

Harry 'Pop' Sherman & Hoppy

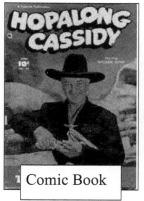

Comic Book

1st film

Club Membership
Birthday Wishes

Cover of Life

Just a Small Sample of
Hopalong Cassidy Merchandising

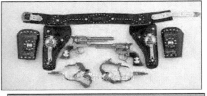

Hoppy through the Years

Four main teamings with Hoppy. Upper left: James Ellison & George Hayes. Right: Russell Hayden & Hayes. Directly left: Andy Clyde & Hayden. Note Hoppy's lighter outfit.
Below: Clyde & Rand Brooks

Boyd would cut this last set of films down to fit a 30 minute time slot for the first 12 shows in the first season on TV

The final 14 in the first season co-starred Edgar Buchanan as Red Connors who went on to play the character in 40 episodes.

The Lone Ranger on Radio

Fran Striker

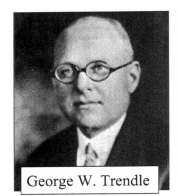

George W. Trendle

George Seaton (Stenius)

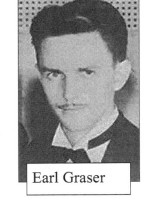

Earl Graser

Brace Beemer

Fred Foy

The Lone Ranger in Serials
and Early Television

Lee Powell

Robert Livingston

Clayton Moore

John Hart

The Legend Continues . . . Sort of

Tex Hill

Klinton Spilsbury

Chad Michael Murray

Armie Hammer

Gene's Empire Expands to Television

The Gene Autry Show

The Range Rider

Annie Oakley

Buffalo Bill. Jr.

The Adventures of Champion

CISCO CLEANS UP FOR TELEVISION

Duncan Renaldo, with moustache, riding a white and
Martin Garralaga as Pancho (Monogram).

Renaldo cleans up and returns as Cisco with paint (Diablo)
and Leo Carrillo as Pancho (United Artists).

The transformation is complete for TV (Ziv).

Those Happy Trails

The Roy Rogers Show had quite a cast of characters, but he only produced one other program. ***Brave Eagle*** with Keith Larson and Kim Winona.

TIMBER CREEK PRESS